Finding Leaders for Tomorrow's Churches

the growing crisis in clergy recruitment

ROY M. OSWALD

an alban institute publication

Grateful acknowledgment is made for use of the following:

Excerpts from "The Hands That Would Shape Our Souls" in *The Atlantic Monthly*, by Paul Wilkes, December 1990. Used by permission.

Excerpts from "Qualities for Ministry," paper from the American Baptist Churches/USA, Board of Educational Ministries, 1988, Valley Forge Headquarters. Used by permission.

BV
4011.4
.089
1993

The Publications Program of The Alban Institute is assisted by a grant from Trinity Church, New York City.

Library of Congress Catalog Card Number 93-73156
ISBN 1-56699-116-1

CONTENTS

PREFACE

On July 9, 1989, the front page of the *New York Times* headlined "Shortage of Qualified New Clergy Causing Alarm for U. S. Religion." The article described a changed seminary universe where the typical candidate profile was increasingly at odds with the needs and expectations of the local congregation.

Is the premise correct? What are the problems? Are there solutions? What has changed in the generation since I attended seminary? My class of 1962 at Luther School of Theology at Chicago was a portrait of homogeneity: young, masculine, invulnerable. Many of us were "preachers' kids," steeped in our denominational traditions, secure in our choice of careers.

In 1962 sensitivity to issues of ageism, sexism, and racism had not yet penetrated our consciousness nor our theology. Later in the decade the Vietnam War, the civil rights struggle, and waves of societal recriminations would wash over all of us. Churches and synagogues would occupy center stage, even though membership rosters would shrink in all but a few denominations.

For us, gaining approval to be ordained was a relatively simple process of application and endorsement and training with none of the rigorous testing of the call that would be instituted in the 1970s.

We did not regard the turning points of entering or graduating from seminary as *dangerous opportunities* (a literal translation of the Chinese words for *crises*). We were confident that our professional and spiritual goals would be attained.

Little did I imagine that I would spend a substantial part of my professional life examining the phenomenon of church-related "boundary crossings." Eighteen years ago with The Alban Institute I studied the "boundary" that clergy cross when they move from one parish to another. (This was the Pastoral Termination and Start-Up Project.) The next boundary we studied was with seminary graduates—as they move from seminary to their first parishes (the Crossing the Boundary Research Project). Our research team interviewed 102 recent seminary graduates from ten institutions representing eight denominations. In 1977 seminaries were beginning to graduate more female candidates, older second-career people, minority and ethnic candidates, and students from unconventional, some would say dysfunctional, academic and family backgrounds. It was clear that these groups were encountering new kinds of obstacles. But we also learned that for most candidates, no matter what their background, screening and placement processes had caused an erosion of confidence and affirmation.

In my subsequent travels I was getting disturbing feedback from hundreds of seminarians, parish clergy, and church executives. Evaluative and screening procedures were viewed as self-defeating. Seminaries and their denominational partners were at odds as to where blame should be assessed. Seminarians often felt abandoned and spiritually bereft.

After conducting a large study on lay people crossing the boundary from nonmembership to membership in a parish (the Assimilation of New Members Project), I was drawn to study another point-of-passage: the boundary at the front end of theological education between the decision to "go" for ordination and ultimate acceptance or rejection.

I am deeply appreciative to The Alban Institute for facilitating my participation in all of these research efforts. I've received an education that could not be paralleled in any academic institution.

In 1987 the Arthur Vining Davis Foundations awarded The Alban Institute a grant for this study—to assess the needs of clergy candidates, seminaries, and the clergy and laypeople serving on middle judicatory committees or commissions that were screening candidates for ordained ministry. This book reports on more than five years of activity involving Alban's contact with twenty-nine middle judicatories, forty-one theological institutions, and fourteen hundred seminarians.

Appendix I gives a research chronology and acknowledgments to all the participants and our team members. However, I want to express my special appreciation to our primary funder, the Arthur Vining Davis Foundations, and to the Board of Theological Education of the Episcopal

Church, which provided matching funds for major elements of our study. I am also grateful to officials at Educational Testing Services and the Lilly Endowment who have shared significant information with me from their important studies now being prepared for publication. Another contributor was the Siebert Foundation, which provided funds for a recruitment study in Wisconsin. Finally, I want to pay tribute to the efforts of particular people whose insights and direct assistance was instrumental in making this project so comprehensive and multidimensional.

This most recent research effort began where all my research projects have begun—in Loren Mead's office. Over the past eighteen years, my time spent with Loren has always been a bonanza of ideas, theories, and potential research. We generate ten times the ideas and projects we can possibly execute. No regrets for that. These have been some of my most enjoyable years—working with The Alban Institute. It will be a sad day for me when he steps down as president of the Institute.

I am grateful to the cadre of church professionals (twenty-three in all) who volunteered time as "think-tank" participants for this project. Many traveled great distances to spend two separate days with us.

Then there was the project team that spent hours interviewing seminary students, search committee members, and middle-judicatory executives in our initial data-gathering probe: Margot Clark, Linda Kramer, Burt Newman, Ed White, Lois Simpson, and Antti Lepisto.

When the Episcopal Church hired us to complete a portion of their study, funded by the Lilly Endowment, I called upon the able assistance of Ellis Larson, a Wesley Seminary faculty member, to help organize the questionnaire that went to more than fourteen hundred seminary students. I especially valued his ability to computerize the results and analyze the data.

When we looked at clergy recruitment and screening from a seminary perspective, I was moved by the evident passion of seminary personnel for this issue. More than thirty representatives of denominational seminaries took time to survey their faculties and then spend a day with us sharing their reflections.

The encouragement of Celia Hahn was a key factor in the writing of this document. And I am most indebted to Julie King, my former administrative assistant, who came out of retirement to bring order and structure to my ramblings. With her writing skills and her breadth of knowledge of church systems, she made a major contribution to this manuscript.

This study has left me with some deep convictions on this subject. You will feel my passion as I attempt to catalog what I have learned from this research. I'd welcome the opportunity to be in dialogue with you and your denomination on this issue. No denomination can fix, once and for all, the problem of clergy recruitment and screening. We need to continue to learn more about this as we try to implement what we have already learned. Yet I remain hopeful that this generation of church leaders has got what it takes to:

- attract vital people to consider the ordained ministry;
- open the door leading to ordination to those who will provide faithful, effective leadership for the church;
- close the door to those who will have a destructive effect on the church; and
- be in confident prayer for the Spirit's guidance as they seek to make the right choices with aspirants who fall between the above poles.

INTRODUCTION

For two decades Roy Oswald has worked at understanding the special gifts and difficulties of the ordained clergy. He has done research, engaged in informal explorations, and led training events for thousands of clergy. Twice a year for ten days he and three dozen outstanding clergy "go deep" in the Clergy Development Institute that he developed and leads for The Alban Institute.

Few people know clergy more deeply, and few are more passionate supporters of clergy.

Supported by a $100,000 grant from the Arthur Vining Davis Foundations, Roy has been able to spend part of the past few years focusing on how clergy candidates are recruited and screened. This project complements his work from 1976-1980, studying the "boundary" that students cross as they leave seminary and go to their first congregations. The Arthur Vining Davis explorations also look at the "boundary" one crosses going into seminary, trying to shed light on what happens as candidates go from their ordinary church life into the seminary.

In the course of these years of focused attention, Roy engaged in a variety of activities to better understand the complex issues involved. The activities ranged from careful gathering of data and manipulation of statistical variables to in-depth personal interviews and focus group discussions. Some parts of the study involved careful research confidential to a particular client. Each phase influenced subsequent phases.

In the final analysis, we have come to describe this series of studies and probings as a focused exploration of a major issue before the churches.

In this book that exploration is presented to you by the one who was at the heart of each part of it—Roy Oswald. This model of study is not objective, distant, or empirical.

In grappling with this book, you will be dealing with a critical issue of the church in the next generation—the selection of those to be trained for professional leadership. Your guide to the exploration is a passionate searcher for knowledge; what he reports is the message to which this search has led him.

In a variety of programs across the country, judicatories and seminaries have used the 1976-1980 "boundary" studies to shape the help seminary graduates receive as they enter congregational ministries. We hope that this book—this report of explorations of the boundary *into* seminary—will similarly help to raise issues, challenge practices, and stimulate new efforts to seek the best candidates as professional leaders of the churches of tomorrow.

Loren B. Mead

CHAPTER I

A Framework for Understanding Our Study

We began our study with a clear vision. To ensure the calibre of leadership needed to stem membership decline and affirm the central position of the religious community in American life, better processes were needed for the selection and recruitment of candidates for the ordained ministry.

Our vision was clear, but the issues were complex and painful. A total system appeared to be in crisis. All levels of the church were affected: congregations, parish clergy, middle-judicatory screening bodies, seminaries, national church offices, and of course the prospective candidates for ordination. Policies and strategies currently in place were diffused among the many subsystems; this complicated our research task.

Over a three-year period my research colleagues and I met with representatives of twenty-six middle judicatories and thirty-one theological institutions. We also had face-to-face interviews with several dozen students and conducted a national survey of 1,297 additional seminarians in 23 schools. Six denominations made up our sample: United Methodist, Episcopal, Evangelical Lutheran Church in America, Reformed Church in America, Presbyterian Church (USA), and United Church of Christ. (We were later able to add information from American Baptists, Christian Church (Disciples of Christ), Lutheran Church—Missouri Synod, and Unitarian-Universalists.)

Our surveys and interviews examined nine functions that each of these denominations incorporates into its candidacy protocol.

1. gaining approval and support from pastor and home congregation;
2. applying to be admitted into the process;
3. interviewing and being endorsed;

4. submitting to psychological testing;
5. being assigned "shepherds" or contact persons;
6. training at a theological institution;
7. carrying out some kind of internship;
8. being evaluated and approved by seminary faculty; and
9. receiving final endorsement leading to ordination.

We soon confirmed that even *within* one denomination these functions might be carried out in vastly different ways. We were confronting not six systems but a multitude. For our own clear understanding and for useful interpretation of our research findings by a wider public, we needed some kind of a road map.

As we analyzed and compared systems in our initial dialogues with seminary and denominational personnel, we found that some systems validated the call to ministry almost exclusively at the congregational level. This might be before or after seminary education. For others, validation took place at the seminary level. In others there was joint oversight by both seminaries and denominational entities.

The map we began to develop had its check points at many different junctures along the highway to ordination and an array of detours and road blocks. We adopted the terms *front-end loading, middle loading,* and *back-end loading* as a way of identifying where greatest emphasis was placed. Certainly all denominations did some work at all three stages, but we felt it would be helpful to identify where greatest effort was expended and how timing might affect outcomes.

Front-end-loading denominations placed a heavy emphasis on screening applicants *before* they were allowed to enter seminary. Middle-loading denominations did their heaviest screening while aspirants were in seminary and in field work. Back-end-loading denominations concentrated screening efforts on the postseminary period.

In our six targeted denominations, we identified two as being front-end loading: United Methodist and Episcopal. Middle loading was most evident in the Evangelical Lutheran Church in America (ELCA). Back-end-loading denominations were the Reformed Church in America (RCA), Presbyterian Church (USA), and United Church of Christ (UCC).

For clarity in comparing one denomination to another, we identified advantages and disadvantages for each of the three loading systems.

Front-End-Loading System

Advantages: Early in the game denominations communicate what is expected of quality aspirants. It is quite clear who is likely to be accepted further down the line. Persons with questionable ability are screened out right from the start. Denominations are then able to be more hopeful about placing seminary graduates once they are in the pipeline.

Disadvantages: The ability, motivation, and commitment of aspirants is judged before these people are given a chance to prove themselves. In some cases, the judgment is made on scanty and superficial data.

Also, compliance with stringent requirements up front, before admission to seminary, may become a kind of hazing process that is most amenable to passive-dependent personality types who are dependent on authority and ready to do whatever is required of them, even though they may feel anger and resentment. Later in this book I will deal with this personality type in ministry.

Stringent front-end-loading systems also tend to lengthen the time of preparation for ministry, adding in some cases an additional two or two-and-one-half years to a three-year seminary training program.

Back-End-Loading System

Advantages: Everyone has free access to a seminary education. Anyone is free to explore the possibilities of a career as an ordained person without facing a lot of stricture. Denominations using this process are then free to call into the ordained ministry those it deems fit from the cadre of seminary graduates.

Disadvantages: The church must place judgment on people who have already committed three or four years of their lives to this particular professional training. Some may have made great sacrifices to put themselves through seminary, especially second-career candidates, with or without spouse and children. Screening committees often do not have the heart to give a firm no to an individual after he or she has committed so much to the process.

In some back-end-loading systems the key to acceptance into the ordained ministry is the ability to receive a call from a local congregation. This forces a congregation to be the arbiter of qualifications for ministry— a great deal to ask of a church where the candidate is not well-known and may not be well-connected.

Middle-Loading System

Advantages: Everyone who entertains the thought of entering the parish ministry may attend at least one year of seminary. During this initial year at seminary a decision is made as to whether the student will be allowed to continue. A second screening takes place during the year of parish internship or during the final year of seminary training. In some denominations it is completely up to the seminary faculty to decide who gets ordained and who does not. In other middle-loading systems, a screening task force is made up of some seminary faculty and some members of the middle judicatory screening committee. A clear advantage of this system is that the people who get to watch a student day in and day out for three years are in on the decision related to the individual's ordination.

Disadvantages: Much emphasis is placed on how well a student does in seminary or how well the aspirant does in the eyes of seminary faculty and administration. Yet some aspirants who do well in a seminary community do not work out well as pastors. In short, academic ability sometimes does not translate into being effective in the role of religious authority.

In some middle-loading systems, heavy emphasis is placed on a full year of internship in a parish setting. This places heavy pressure on aspirants in situations where heads-of-staff may not be ideal mentors.

A further concern is whether seminary faculty members carrying ultimate power-of-decision are sufficiently in touch with the realities of parish ministry to make such decisions or whether denominational politics may make this responsibility uncomfortable. Additionally, when the survival of a seminary depends upon having students, conflict of interest is bound to be present. Most mainline Protestant denominations have too many seminaries given their need for graduates.

Overview

As you can see, all systems have both advantages and disadvantages. As we began our work, our intention was to identify the most positive features of each of the separate processes and to present opportunities for denominations to learn from one another.

Yet we found ourselves confronting many special cases. Even though criteria for calling candidates to ministry were often addressed by national bodies, the criteria were being interpreted and carried out by local or regional decision makers. Most such middle-level bodies were overwhelmed by the complexity and scope of their responsibilities, their lack of clarity, absence of training and team-cohesiveness, and rotating membership.

A further dilemma was that most of the denominations in our study were confronting a quality and quantity impasse: (1) more applicants than their systems could wisely use and (2) few candidates of the high quality they believed they needed.

As you read on, you will find that we have organized our findings around the various constituencies: seminarians; seminary deans, faculty, and admissions officers; the clergy and laity carrying out endorsement and application functions; and middle-judicatory bishops, executives, and staffs. We have tried to provide a balanced reflection of what these people told us.

We then turn to problem areas or "pinch points" where there is strong disagreement among the various players; in these areas there may have been a breakdown in trust and feelings of resentment and anxiety. *Passive* and *reactive* are two words commonly used to describe current models for recruiting and screening candidates for ministry. We review our own findings and information from other research to test the accuracy of assumptions about the seriousness of the situation.

Finally, we offer examples of new thinking on candidacy processes from both national and local initiatives. Some of these models are already being implemented; others are "on hold" because of fiscal constraints.

I have witnessed the talent and leadership ability to bring about change, but a broad-based consensus and a shared vision are needed. Who will lead the way? Answering that question has been the purpose of this exploration.

CHAPTER II

The Seminarians

In the United States and Canada, 208 institutions are accredited by the Association of Theological Schools. These schools enrolled just under sixty thousand students in the fall of 1991, which represented a very slight increase (1.2 percent) over the previous year. Full-time enrollment declined from 76 percent to 65 percent.[1]

In the past five years intense research has focused on today's seminary population. Starting in 1987 the Lilly Endowment provided five million dollars to a number of church organizations and theological institutions to explore ways to enlarge and improve the next generation of American clergy.

The Alban Institute was able to participate in this research effort by completing a study for the Board for Theological Education of the Episcopal Church. This work complemented our inquiries into other denominations—underwritten by the Arthur Vining Davis Foundations and other contributors. A major piece of our study was directed to how seminarians had experienced the call, what their church involvement and theological perspectives were, and how they felt about the requirements of their candidacy systems.

Alban's research sample included forty-eight Episcopal seminarians extensively interviewed and 1,297 students (one-third Episcopal, two-thirds non-Episcopal) who responded to a ten-page survey.[2] They represented twenty-three institutions of six denominations: Christian Church (Disciples of Christ), Episcopal, Evangelical Lutheran Church in America (ELCA), United Methodist, Presbyterian Church (USA), and United Church of Christ (UCC). (For a summary of the research design, see Appendix I.)

Some noteworthy findings emerged.

1. Almost 40 percent of respondents came from either Family-sized (50 or fewer active members) or Pastoral (51-150 active) congregations.

2. Sizable numbers affirmed support for their call from a variety of non-church people: spouses (87 percent), counselors (66 percent), campus ministers (64 percent), parents (61 percent).

3. The determination to pursue the call, regardless of denominational advice, was stronger among older (40+) seminarians; only one-fifth of this group would investigate alternatives, compared to one-third of the under-forty respondents.

4. Twenty-seven percent of the seminarians reported a "single" marital status; 50 percent were in their first marriages; 23 percent were separated, divorced, or widowed.

Information released up to this time by Educational Testing Service (Princeton, NJ) from its Lilly-funded studies has addressed demographic characteristics and academic preparation. Here are some salient facts from that study about today's seminarians.

1. Between 1972 and 1987 there was a fivefold increase in the number of women preparing for ordination.[3]

2. Almost 40 percent of the Educational Testing Service (ETS) seminary sample had been engaged in two or more types of work before admission.[4]

3. The average age of entering seminarians rose by almost ten years between 1965 and 1990.[5]

4. From 1981 to 1987, women scored twenty-four points higher than men on the verbal section of the Graduate Record Examinations.[6]

This sampling of ETS and Alban findings underscores the marked changes in seminary populations over the past two decades. Joseph

O'Neill and Richard Murphy, ETS researchers, believe that the demographic profile of the North American seminarian has changed more in those twenty years than in the prior two hundred years.[7]

The remainder of this chapter will expand on six aspects of the characteristic seminarian profile: academic qualifications; family and religious background; age and career expectations; gender, race, and sexual preference; marital and financial status; and feelings toward the church.

Academic Qualifications

A major concern expressed these days is that the church is no longer attracting "the brightest and the best." ETS researchers looked at the academic credentials of twelve thousand applicants to M.Div. programs who had taken the Graduate Record Examinations (GREs) between 1981 and 1988. The GRE has three separate sections: verbal, quantitative, and analytical. ETS noted that verbal scores for its sample ranged over the entire spectrum, and gender differences were marked. For example, 33 percent of the women but only 19 percent of the men had verbal scores of six hundred or higher (out of eight hundred).

ETS researchers also compared the 1987 GRE verbal score averages from their sample with U.S. citizens planning to do graduate work in the humanities and helping professions. The average of all examination-takers was 505; for prospective M.Div. candidates the average was 493. Thirteen intended fields of study ranked higher than the M.Div. group.[8]

Certainly academic rankings are not the most reliable predictors of success in ministry. The GRE is not required by most seminaries that use other criteria for determining admission. The ETS research team noted how little concrete information seminaries and judicatories have on academic strengths and weaknesses.

One of the participants in Alban's initial research conference to prepare the candidacy study was Dr. L. Guy Mehl, director of the Lancaster Career Development Center. Over the past twenty years, he has worked with 1,400 candidates for ministry from a variety of denominations. Here is what he has observed.

Academic capability [in aspiring clergy] has diminished in the last fifteen years. On one of our tests, which measures advanced, academic English, the difference between candidates and clergy of the last fifteen years and clergy who are in their late fifties and older is that the mean is 16 points lower for the new group (half a standard deviation). This means a significant reduction in advanced language skills. New clergy will not be able to write as well, understand the subtleties of their native tongue, or handle concepts imbedded in their native language as well as older clergy. One can expect that theological subtleties and distinctions will not be grasped as quickly and that language will not be as beautiful a tool as it was for former generations of clergy.[9]

Family and Religious Background

One difference between today's seminarians and their predecessors appears to be true regardless of denomination, gender, or age: They are less thoroughly grounded in their religious traditions. Daniel Aleshire, director of professional studies at the Southern Baptist Seminary in Louisville, told the *New York Times* that only half of the seminarians coming into his denomination's theological institutions were Baptist-college graduates. Many had had religious awakenings in their older years.[10]

Today you can no longer assume a common background in seminarians. People entering theological institutions have not absorbed the cultural patterns and the subtle and informal ways things are accomplished in a particular denomination. A perspective on this phenomenon among Jewish candidates was offered by Rabbi Neil Gillman of the Jewish Theological Seminary. He noted that many of his students had not been raised in the religious tradition they now proposed to study.

> The students want authenticity, because they have been exposed to so much phoniness, but they are on the periphery. They want the authenticity of Judaism and yet want to be able to pick and choose, be free to accept or reject aspects of Judaism—which puts them exactly where most of their congregations are. What differentiates them, raises them up in this secular time, is not only that they want an inner focus to their life...but that they are now seeking it through

religious beliefs. By the time they come here they are religious, but not necessarily observant.[11]

Yet there is evidence that many of those who pursue other interests after college before coming to seminary have been personally active in their local congregational leadership. Lilly-funded studies at Union Theological Seminary and Colgate Rochester Divinity School identified numbers of highly capable students who had not come from the customary recruitment pool. What almost all of them had in common was personal involvement in church life.[12]

In Alban's nationwide survey we found that 71 percent of Episcopal and 59 percent of non-Episcopal seminarians described home church involvement as "very active."

My own informal study notes a dramatic decline in the number of "preachers' kids" pursuing a career in the church. Whenever I give a workshop for clergy (more than a hundred a year), I gather some data at the beginning. In a differentiation exercise I have participants walk to different parts of the room, depending on their answers to the question at hand. When I ask how many of them had an ordained father, younger clergy rarely move forward. Next I ask: "How many of you have children who are entering or have entered the ordained ministry?" Painfully few give a positive response.

In the 1950s and 1960s it was common for children to follow the career path of their clergy parents. These second-generation clerics brought many built-in advantages to the role. They were much more in touch with the human side of parish ministry and knew how to balance professional and personal life. While growing up they had observed how their clergy parents managed certain parish difficulties and problems.

I suspect that some traumatic experiences have persuaded clergy to discourage their own children from entering the profession. Other factors might be the decline in respect for the role, the low pay, the long hours, and the heartaches.

When we interviewed seminary faculty, one of the recurring comments was the sense that students were biblically illiterate and totally uninformed about the history of their denominations.

The findings from our nationwide survey, however, highlighted a countervailing phenomenon. One-third of the respondents described themselves as theologically conservative and as coming from conservative congregations. It is probably accurate to say that these people connect to the Gospel and exhibit energy for witness and outreach.

My belief is that more conservative, evangelical candidates survive the highly demanding front-end-loading systems. They convey a conviction and clarity about their religious convictions and sense of call from God.

There is a good deal of conjecture these days about how family backgrounds shape candidacy and early ministry. In a later chapter, I will spend more time on this subject; for now, here is what Guy Mehl of the Lancaster Career Center believes.

This generation of seminarians, it seems to me, will be heavily composed of rescuers who are driven by co-dependent needs. Coming from dysfunctional families, as so many of them do, and having grown up rescuing within these families, they will be natural rescuers in church settings.

Whether this is good or bad depends upon your point of view. What is reasonable to say, though, is that vigorous assertive leadership for the church in this new generation of clergy will be in shorter supply. Co-dependency carries with it insecurity and uncertainty. These candidates will be counselors and chaplains more than they will be theologians and leaders.[13]

The issue of emotional and psychological preparation for ministry is further complicated by the age, gender, race, sexual preference, and marital status of today's seminarians.

Age of Seminarians

The percentage of men under the age of thirty in the ETS sample dropped from 86 percent in 1977 to 63 percent in 1987.[14] Alban's 1989 seminary survey showed that among female and male candidates, only one in five were under age thirty. For some critics of today's candidacy process, this is cause for great alarm. For others, it is a positive indication of more extensive life experience.

Another perception is that the heavy influx of second-career personnel into the candidacy process is simply because we are attracting people unable to achieve success in secular careers. This conclusion is rejected by Ellis L. Larsen, professor of church administration at Wesley Theological Seminary, who was able to study a nationwide sample of these older seminarians. He claims that older seminarians exhibit much the same motivation as the younger ones and an even greater degree of self-confidence. He feels that the second-career person brings a wealth of personal experience to the ministry and has already resolved many personal issues.[15]

Those setting policies at the national level are particualrly apprehensive about pressures on pension funds and difficulties in accommodating the persistent call for young, male clergy.

The Episcopal Board for Theological Education provides a balanced response to the question "How old should seminarians be?" It concludes:

> Using the age of aspirants as a criterion for selection...seems to be highly ambiguous. "Ageism," no matter what end of the continuum is favored or discriminated against, seems no more fitting for vocational testing than for secular job placement. Given the statistics, however, it seems essential that the church find ways to encourage at least a higher percentage of applicants of more youthful age.[16]

Significantly, the health field has also experienced a surge in older applicants. Between 1981 and 1991 there was a 23 percent increase in people twenty-eight and older admitted to medical schools. (These older students appeared to be more likely to go into primary care.)[17]

One thing is clear. Mainline Protestant churches are not receiving nearly the number of younger applicants to ministry as in former years. There are some heavy-duty implications in this. Older seminarians will not be serving the church for nearly as long a period of time as their younger counterparts. This means the church will need to go to the same expense of training them for ministry, and yet receive ten, twenty, or thirty fewer years of service from them. It has also exacerbated the whole issue of the clergy shortage about to hit us. Does this mean we should be accepting twice as many candidates for ministry—as they will be serving only half as long?

The declining birthrate between 1967 and 1976 may already be altering the age curve once again. As the ETS researchers point out, the combination of the "baby bust" demographics and denominational policies is unlikely to lower the average age of seminarians.

Gender, Race, and Sexual Preference

The average age of first-year female seminarians has been consistently higher than that of men, and, as already noted, there has been a fivefold increase in women preparing for ordination.

Virtually all seminary educators agree that the first large group of women to enter seminaries in the 1970s was unusually capable and highly motivated. Only the influx of women kept the shortage of talented seminarians from being much graver. This was brought home to me visually when I happened to pick up the Lancaster Seminary alumni newspaper, which showed pictures and credentials of the entire graduating class of 1986. Of the thirty-plus graduates that year, about one-third were women. Four women graduated magna cum laude and another five graduated cum laude. Only three males that year graduated cum laude, and none of the males graduated magna cum laude.

Yet sadly, most of the men in that class had little trouble receiving their first calls to parish ministry, while it was a different story for the women. The bias against women in ministry remains tenacious. But given the talent of many of these women, it may simply be a matter of time. As one man who had just served on the congregational calling committee said to me, "When we got right down to it, the female candidate we called was head and shoulders more talented than any of the men we interviewed."

The *Yearbook of American and Canadian Churches* confirmed that in 1991, for the first time, more than 30 percent of seminarians were women. For an extended exploration of the subject of female candidates, see chapter 6.

African-American seminary enrollment has continued at a steady pace with an average 5.6 percent increase each year for the past five years. Still, blacks made up only 7.6 percent of the total seminary enrollment in 1991, and in some denominations that figure was significantly lower. (Pacific/Asian-Americans entered theological institutions at a faster rate than any other ethnic constituency during the past fourteen years, but Hispanic enrollment declined in 1991 for the first time in five years.)[18]

In our interviews we found a great paradox when we looked at the recruitment and screening processes of denominations from the point of view of racial and ethnic minorities. The clear majority of denominations we studied held as a high value cultural and ethnic diversity. Most saw racial diversity as the cutting edge of their growth and vitality. Yet all of the systems we studied complained about the lack of minority aspirants applying for candidacy within their systems. The absence of black and Hispanic applicants was most troublesome to these screening committees.

The Princeton Research Center for the Study of Religion proposes that blacks and Hispanics are more likely to respond to invitations and overtures of church membership than whites.

> Members of minority groups do not feel alienated from the churches. Only 8 percent of blacks and 3 percent of Hispanics say they have ever felt unwelcome or excluded from any church because of their race or ethnicity....
>
> Blacks (69 percent) are considerably more likely than whites (52 percent) or Hispanics (57 percent) to say that religion is "very important" to them.[19]

Given this evidence of strong religious commitment, it should disturb us that we have such a hard time encouraging blacks and Hispanics to consider a vocation in ordained ministry.

If we were able to effectively recruit minority candidates, what might their experiences in parish placement be?

An edition of the Washington Episcopal Clergy Association (WECA) newsletter provides perspectives on minority deployment in the Northeast Region of the Episcopal Church. These notes from the Reverend Kevin Matthews relate to the year 1989 and may have altered somewhat since then.

> There are only about 280 active Black clergy of whom about 25 are active Black female clergy. There are only seven Black clergy as rectors of predominantly white congregations. Less than 20 Blacks are currently enrolled in Episcopal seminaries....When Black clergy began moving into a wider variety of positions, it was not to... parishes but to specialized ministries.[20]

Kevin Matthews's summation in the newsletter was poignant: "Minority clergy are struggling in a system not set up for them."

In an interview at a large urban judicatory in the South, we talked

about the critical need for black applicants. But none had completed
the extended screening process then in place. This process had not been
instituted to exclude minority applicants. The system had been put in
place as a rational way to deal with an overloaded admissions situation.
It reminded me of a speech by Barbara Wheeler, president of Auburn
Theological Seminary, in which she posed the question "What Kind of
Leadership for Tomorrow's Churches?" Here is what she had to say
about a "systems approach" to the church's admissions needs.

> The systems approach is not designed to uncover and promote...
> qualities of leadership. The systems way of thinking prompts us to
> ask of the applicants....Will she fit into the system?...It does *not*
> prompt us to ask—indeed it discourages us from asking: How ori-
> ginal and creative is this person? What is unique about her? What
> will she bring to the church that it not only lacks but doesn't even
> know it lacks?[21]

Barbara Wheeler goes on to point out that an admissions focus on
rules, requirements, procedures, and tests sends a message that the needs
of the system take precedence over the value of individuals.

Mainline denominations continue to wonder why they have such
indifferent success in attracting minorites into the ministry. If they examine their systems with new eyes, they may begin to understand what it
is like for any newcomer, but perhaps particularly for a minority newcomer, to ask for entrance.

Another point of confusion and mistrust is over the ordination of
homosexual people. As I complete this book, resolution of the Clinton
administration's efforts to draft new rules affecting gays and lesbians
in the military is in doubt. This controversy evokes all the hubbub of
debates in the various denominations over the past decade. The Reverend Richard McBrien, chairman of Notre Dame's theology department,
framed his denomination's dilemma in this way.

> What impact does the presence of a large number of gay seminarians
> have on the spiritual tone and moral atmosphere of our seminaries?
> ...How many heterosexual seminarians have decided to leave the
> seminary and abandon their interest in a presbyterial vocation
> because of the presence of significant numbers of gays in seminaries
> and among the local clergy?[22]

The Reverend John Coleman, a sociologist at the Jesuit School of
Theology at Berkeley, says, "I'm sure that gay people make good priests.
But when a disproportionate number of priests, even if chaste, have a
different sexual orientation than the population they serve, this is a
serious issue."[23]

The Roman Catholic experience may spring from unusual pressures
on those who screen applicants because of the dramatic shortage of
priests. But these doubts and arguments continue to surface at regional
and national Protestant conclaves.

The ambivalence expresses itself in the recruiting and screening
processes of each denomination as aspirants either have to risk being
rejected or be dishonest regarding their own personal sexual history or
viewpoint when it differs from the church's party line. According to our
study, each time aspirants need to go underground on an issue, more
anger and diillusionment toward the church accumulates.

Marital and Financial Status

As reported earlier, our seminary survey showed 23 percent of students
who identified themselves as separated, divorced, or widowed. The ETS
study has looked at divorce rates among female seminarians and found
them comparable to the rate in the general population (21.2 per thousand).[24]

That study also confirms that at any given age female seminarians
are more likely than males to be widowed or divorced. The older they
are when entering seminary, the greater the likelihood that they are
divorced. An interesting sidelight is that the number of female and male
seminarians reporting divorce of parents more than doubled between
1975 and 1990.

The relevance of this information on divorce is that it fortifies a
perception of today's applicants as more vulnerable and less well balanced personally. The notion that women generally enter the ministry
because of some trauma feeds a sexist stereotype that has, according to
our interviews, caused some middle judicatories to declare moratoria on
older female candidates.

Another worry is the financial crunch experienced by most applicants.
As a generalization, present-day seminarians and candidates are very

stressed financially. We are talking here about people graduating from seminary fifteen to twenty thousand dollars in debt. This is frequently an accumulation of undergraduate debt, living expenses, and seminary costs. Seminaries are also being stretched financially, so their costs are rising quickly, contributing to this problem. At Berkeley Divinity School, tuition and housing for one person is estimated at $17,500 per year. No loan was available for more than $7,500.

The pattern of a male seminarian with a working professional wife (often in education or nursing) was the norm some years ago. Today's seminary student is more likely to be single, a second-career person with one or more dependents, a single parent, or a married student without a professionally trained spouse. Only the student with a professionally employed spouse is in an economically favorable situation.

The financial plight of seminarians may not seem as dramatic as that of new medical school graduates, who now enter their profession with an average debt of $46,224.[25] But, there is no comparison between the average annual income of physicians and of clergy.

Seminarians' Attitudes toward the Church

I began this chapter by observing that in the past five years there had been an intense research focus on seminarians. Much of that research has been statistical. While these figures are very helpful, I find the ideas and attitudes that came through in our correspondence and interviews equally compelling.

These people were viewing the church-as-a-whole through the prism of their candidacy and seminary experiences. The "war stories" they shared from whatever screening system they had experienced fueled uncertainties about the politics of their denominations.

When asked whether graduation from a seminary should *not* be a necessary requirement for ordination, a significant number of students agreed. We discovered that this group was dominated by older students.

Almost one-third of our respondents felt that it was not safe to be truly open in the screening process, but an overwhelming majority did feel that psychological testing was appropriate.

As to the seminary itself, some students had expected it to be much more of a spiritual community. They expected to have someone offering them spiritual direction and were surprised when there was so little interest in their prayer life. Others were disappointed with the quality of community life. They wanted it to be affirming but found it to be political, particularly as they viewed in-fighting among faculty members.

Some women expected their schools to be more inclusive and to value feminist perspectives. They were disillusioned by the plight of women who had been ordained and were now struggling to receive second and third calls.

Commuter students were having the most difficulty trying to fit into seminary life. Outside jobs and family obligations exacerbated the pressures. Yet many reported empathic contacts with faculty and strong friendships developing with fellow students. Our research team felt that those with whom they spoke did value their schools and did express lasting loyalties.

It seemed apparent from our conversations that seminarians would have had fewer surprises if their screening committees and/or advisors had provided more transitional assistance. Screening committees would also do well to show ongoing concern about the spiritual lives of their candidates. In a later chapter dealing with denominational candidacy processes, I will return to how this kind of shepherding relationship could be nurtured.

CHAPTER III

The Seminaries

As part of our five-year research effort, we invited seminary faculty and administrators to meetings held at Auburn Seminary in New York City and the Pacific School of Religion in San Francisco. Before participating in a day-long debriefing, thirty-nine people representing thirty institutions completed a three-page questionnaire based on discussions with seminary colleagues. (For the names of institutions, see the research summary in Appendix I.) Our research team also did intensive on-site interviews at four Episcopal seminaries.

In this group of institutions, eight were nondenominational or multi-denominational. There appeared to be a subtle competition between nondenominational and denominational schools, as well as among those within the same denomination. This is not surprising, given the fact that all seminaries need students to survive; they may be competing for applicants from the same pool.

Seminaries with students of only one denomination are in a minority. Even denominational schools often include students of other denominations. This has changed in the last ten years, with denominations allowing aspirants to be trained in seminaries representing other denominations, thus allowing more students to acquire a seminary education without relocating their spouses and families. The massive influx of second-career students has also changed seminary life considerably, as many continue to hold down part- or full-time jobs while attending local seminaries.

Professional Pressures

Today's seminaries are places of high stress. Gone are the days when a seminary professor could become a world-renowned specialist in one field, teach two or three classes a week, spend the majority of his or her time honing that specialty, and take a year sabbatical every seven years to write a book or become more grounded in a particular field.

Our conference participants described how, as members of relatively small faculties, they must devote significant time and energy to meetings and committees that shape the school's life. They serve as advisors, counselors, and mentors for students. Many are full partners in the candidacy process of their denominations. Increasingly they are involved in recruitment and development. They serve on study commissions and task forces of the church and make formal responses to ecclesiastical documents. Many faculty members also lecture widely and contribute original scholarship through writing. In short, most faculty members are overextended, constantly being pulled away from their areas of expertise and carrying out tasks that do not suit them well.

Economic Pressures

In general, seminary faculty members are overworked and underpaid. A 1991 study of 159 faculty members within the new Evangelical Lutheran Church in America revealed this salary range.

   7.5 percent earned less than $25,000.
   61 percent earned between $25,000 and $40,000.
   31.4 percent earned between $40,000 and $44,000.[1]

That is not a lot of money for someone who has possibly accumulated debt not only from college and seminary, but also from three or four years of postgraduate study.

Behind these stories of understaffed, overworked, and underpaid seminary faculty and administrators is the sharp decline in direct support these seminaries are receiving from their denominations. Across the board, denominations have experienced serious financial cut backs because of rising costs, increased salary needs, and a drop in financial gifts to regional and national church agencies.

All mainline Protestant churches have experienced a steady decline in membership since the early 1970s. Most claim they have stemmed the tide, yet losses have been substantial. Between 1965 and 1975 the Episcopal Church lost 20 percent of its members. The decline among Lutherans was 22 percent, and Methodists lost 11 percent. In the subsequent decade these losses abated somewhat and were only in single digits.[2]

As congregations feel the financial crunch, they are less willing and able to contribute benevolence dollars to their national churches. One place national budgets have been cut is in their direct support of denominational seminaries. Only those seminaries with heavy endowments are able to take these cuts in stride. Direct support for seminaries in the Presbyterian Church (USA) has dropped to 5 percent of operating budgets. The Episcopal Church does not provide direct national support, but asks congregation to give 1 percent of their budgets to the Episcopal seminary of their choice. That method raised three million dollars for eleven seminaries in 1989.

In the newly formed ELCA, grants to seminaries in 1988 were expected to be $9,734,350 and increase by 3 percent annually. Instead, that figure dropped by half a million in 1989 and a million in 1990. Income from synod and churchwide sources, which represented 40 percent of seminaries' budgets in 1989, dropped to 34 percent in 1990. Over the past five years, Lutheran seminaries have been spending capital from their endowments ranging from 6.5 to 8.9 percent. Cambridge Associates (financial consulting firm engaged by a task force studying these seminary transitions) recommends that institutions spend not more than 5 percent of the market value of their endowments. These seminaries are also borrowing from the future by deferring needed maintenance of buildings, furnishings, and equipment.[3]

The decline in financial support from denominational sources continues to weaken the primary and formal links between each system and its seminaries. Increasingly seminaries must seek other sources of funding.

Robert Wood Lynn has expressed a particular concern in the book *Good Stewardship: A Handbook for Seminary Trustees:*

A new round of fiscal anxiety seems to be in the making during the 1990s. If this worrisome trend continues throughout the decade, one can expect some schools to be seduced into a promiscuous search for new programs that will attract tuition-paying students. Even the best schools will be putting more pressure upon already beleagured admissions officers to find students.[4]

As seminaries are increasingly more tuition- and market-driven, their visions can no longer encompass the needs of particular churches for whom specialized kinds of leadership is critical (i.e., inner-city, rural, ethnic). Moreover rising tuition fees will add to student debt and the pressure on graduates to seek well-paying positions—which may not be at the mission frontier of the church. Higher tuitions also may exclude minority candidates or other capable students with limited financial means.

All these pressures are contributing to increased tensions between denominations and their seminaries. We were told that the alienation between church systems and seminaries appears to be increasing rather than diminishing at a time when partnerships are so important.

The solution often put forward is to close seminaries. Closing a seminary is like asking a family to give up its favorite pet. Even though clergy like to criticize seminaries, loyalty among alumni remains strong and deep-rooted.

Each denominational seminary has a regional constituency. Here is how Robert Wood Lynn described the Presbyterian experience.

> Originally this denomination's leaders conceived of establishing one national school to serve the churches and the country. Yet within twenty years after the founding of Princeton Theological Seminary in 1812, regional pride, church politics, and doctrinal differences had spawned the creation of seven competitors. Once established, those schools exhibited a passion for survival. And so the Presbyterians came to know the hidden costs of American pluralism.[5]

Lynn's solution is to foster interdependence among seminaries and to establish networks of seminaries in urban centers or particular regions.

Relationships with Judicatories

Another solution put forward for the survival of seminaries is that they do their own recruiting and screening of potential candidates. At our conferences we heard how some had begun the process of recruiting students not interested in seeking ordination at the conclusion of seminary education. But this proposal would only add to the tension felt between denominations and seminaries.

As we met with screening committees, we frequently heard complaints that they were receiving applications for certification from persons who were already halfway through their seminary training. Committee members did not feel comfortable confronting someone who may have already sacrificed considerable time and resources being trained for ordained ministry.

At our East- and West-Coast seminary meetings almost all the participants confirmed that there was disjuncture among denominational policies, congregational needs, and the needs of their institutions. Screening committee appraisals of students often differed from those of seminary staff. Those qualities valued by screening committees and seminaries frequently did not match the congregational profile of an ideal clergyperson. Aspirants became trapped in this disjuncture with inadequate support and backing.

Seminary faculty and administrators were generally critical of their denominations' screening and recruitment efforts. For denominations that demanded much of their aspirants before allowing them to attend seminary, faculty found these procedures generally ineffective and counterproductive. They felt stringent front-end-loading systems created great stress for the aspirants, generally weeded out the best students as well as the worst, and produced wounded and angry students. Most had nowhere to go with their anger. These systems tended to make students more passive-dependent, or they simply allowed through their systems more passive-dependent students than was healthy for the church.

There was also some faculty dissatisfaction in denominations that did not do much screening up front. These faculty members often felt that committees had an uncritical eagerness to send anyone to seminary—in hope that the seminary would transform a candidate into an effective cleric.

Our conference participants clearly preferred a simplified, informal screening system with minimal requirements until ordination. They identified advantages and disadvantages of such a system.

Advantages: (1) minimal stress on students and faculty; (2) allows students freedom for religious quest; (3) students can test the role of parish pastor without making commitment; (4) emphasizes self-selection and self-screening.

Disadvantages: (1) students are left hanging until approved for ordination; (2) students might be surprised by the requirements for ministry; (3) in some systems congregations are forced to make final ordination decisions.

In spite of these disadvantages, this group of seminary faculty and administrators favors a shorter, simpler process in which a quicker yes or no could be given to aspirants. Once these students were sanctioned, the system could get on with the work of supporting them in the task of developing skills and abilities for ministry.

The clear majority of these seminary representatives felt they were receiving far too many borderline or emotionally wounded students. Was the church expecting the seminary to work miracles? They felt local congregations were blaming them for not adequately preparing ordinands, yet these same congregations were not sending them quality people to work with in the first place.

Here is how the director of one D. Min. program summed up the comments at the meeting he attended.

> It was difficult to discover where students entering seminary were coming from. Even those seminaries which once relied on fairly regularized "feeder systems" noted that these had broken down. Students seemed to arrive at seminary with less clarity about vocation, with many personal issues high on their agendas...and with less time and more entanglements beyond seminary walls. While some students academically were exceptional...others were marginal, and many had little or no theological-religious training.

These people also felt that more training was necessary for clergy and laity to serve on screening committees. Generally they felt these committees were ill-equipped to manage the task of screening people for the ordained ministry.

The majority of the conference participants expressed a strong aversion to participating in evaluation of their students. This time-consuming task was unrewarding because it placed them in an adversarial role in a climate unconducive to learning and growth.

Most faculty want to be friends and advocates for their students. They do not want to be the final arbitrators of their students' careers in the church. Many feel it is a violation of the trust the student places in them when they are required to write a report to the church on anything except the student's academic achievements. As a result, these evaluations tend to be rather superficial, unless extreme behavior norms have been violated, in which case the seminary needs to inform the middle-judicatory screening committee.

In collecting data on how evaluation and feedback tasks are carried out, we discovered a vast array of models—everything from standardized forms to student self-evaluations. I will have more to say on this subject in a later chapter dealing with the role of middle judicatories.

To put it simply, in the economics of seminary existence, seminaries need students to survive. When their enrollments diminish, they have decreased income through tuitions; more important, they have difficulty raising money from other funders. When your survival depends on your seminary having an abundance of students, are you in the best position to judge whether or not a given student is fit to continue in ministerial studies?

Twelve years ago in the pages of The Alban Institute's *Action Information,* John Fletcher reported on a study of sixteen Protestant seminaries. As I conclude this portion of the report on our candidacy study, I would like to evoke a vision he proposed.

Let us imagine a graduation service for a seminary one hundred years from now. Rather than only one group, a faculty, attesting to the academic fitness of the student, there will be two other groups represented, and these three groups will show signs of having worked closely together. The student will have demonstrated his or her personal integrity and promise as a leader in a congregation, and lay and clergy leaders who know the student intimately will be present to witness to all that the student has won their trust and confidence.[6]

CHAPTER IV

Pastors and Congregations

There were limitations to the research design for our study of recruitment and screening. We were able to schedule meetings with scores of clergy and laypeople serving on and staffing regional commissions and committees. But we did not have sufficient resources to connect our data gathering to the local congregations, the formal sponsorship or informal support of which is so critical in the candidacy process.

Nonetheless, on an ad hoc basis, we have learned a great deal about pastoral and congregational roles. These vary widely depending on where the greatest emphasis is placed in a particular denomination.

Approval of Aspirants

It makes clear sense that anyone aspiring to enter the ordained ministry should first receive the backing and support of the home congregation and home pastor. In fact, this should be the toughest examination to pass, as these are the people who know the aspirant best and have some sense as to whether or not this person would make an effective parish pastor.

In the United Methodist Church, a person desiring endorsement first of all contacts the home pastor who then informs the district superintendent. Once the person has been interviewed by the district superintendent, the aspirant must also go before a local Pastor-Parish Relations Committee and then the congregation's annual charge conference to gain approval. The local pastor also must give approval.

In the Episcopal Church, the aspirant needs to gain approval of his

or her rector and vestry. In some dioceses a member of the diocesan
Commission on Ministry meets with the rector and vestry to assist them
in setting up a parish discernment committee. This committee meets
with the aspirant to explore whether the call is to holy orders or to some
other kind of ministry as yet undefined or validated. Critical to the functioning of this committee is the guidance and direction provided by a
trained person on the diocesan level.

In the Presbyterian Church (USA), an advisor meets with the session
to explain its roles and responsibilities in the "preparation for ministry"
process. The session appoints a person to serve as liaison between the
presbytery committee and the potential inquirer once the inquirer has
completed the interview with the session. The session must recommend
that the presbytery enroll the person as an inquirer.

In the Reformed Church in America, the aspirant needs initial approval from the home congregation and is further asked to keep the
congregation informed as to mailing address, study plans, concerns, and
needs. (In many of the systems, once an aspirant has been received into
the process, the home congregation no longer hears from her or him.)

When a member of the United Church of Christ wants to prepare for
ordained ministry, the congregation forms a committee—the pastor and
lay members—to help the member thoroughly explore this decision. The
committee determines if the local church and pastor will recommend the
person to the association for "in-care" status. Because the local church
will make the final recommendation that the person be ordained, the congregation commits itself to a lengthy relationship to the aspirant. Each
congregation is to decide how it can best maintain this relationship and
be supportive to its candidate.

Application for Acceptance

In a congregational system such as the UCC, the application for endorsement comes from the entire congregation. This seems to stimulate the
congregation's investment in the aspirant.

In more hierarchical systems, such as Lutheran, Episcopal, or
Methodist, the local pastor writes a letter of application to the denomination. In the Presbyterian Church (USA) the pastor and the session inform
the Committee on Preparation for Ministry.

In all these systems it is important for the pastor to lead in the effort
to clarify the candidate's gifts and motivations. Two 1990 studies produced interesting perspectives on the influence of pastors in stimulating
the candidacy process. Hartley Hall at Union Theological Seminary in
Virginia analyzed data on the age when ministry was first considered and
when a seminary decision was made. He reported:

> There was a time when calls to ministry typically developed during
> high school and college. Now the arena for ministerial recruitment
> has largely shifted from the campus to the congregation...and the
> local pastor and session have become the primary agents in this all-
> important process.[1]

A 1990 Christian Church (Disciples of Christ) inquiry into formative
influences leading to ministry showed that a pastor had been most influential for 83 percent of black females, 69 percent of white males, 53
percent of black males, and 20 percent of white females.[2]

Support versus Discernment

It is my view that we in the church mistakenly believe we can have both
functions—support and discernment—emanate from the same group of
people. I am skeptical here. Either your function is to support the aspirant trying to make his or her way through the system, or your function
is to help the aspirant critically discover whether the ordained ministry is
appropriate or desired. It is best if two separate persons or groups be
identified, one for each function.

I particularly liked one model among those we encountered in our
interviews. Someone from the middle judicatory helps the local congregation set up a discernment committee and directs the committee as to
how it might reflect with the aspirant the nature of the call. Though
helping a person become clear about the nature of a call is in the long run
a supportive role, it will not feel very supportive in the middle of the
process. Some tough questions need to be asked, such as:

> Why do you need to be ordained to do your ministry?
> What makes you think you can be a good pastor?

How do you know this is a genuine call from God?

Do you have what it takes to stand up to a cantankerous congregation such as ours?

Where have you felt you have exercised strong leadership in the past?

Do you have the physical and emotional stamina to take on this kind of tough role in the church?

How would you decribe your gifts of ministry?

Because church fights are a common thing these days, how do you feel you will stand up to all this conflict?

How would you describe your conflict-management style?

Are you able to afford the expense of seminary training, considering the low salary clergy generally receive?

What clergy models have you admired, and how do you see yourself as similar to or different from them?

Even though friends are asking these questions, they may not seem so friendly at the time. In fact, serious discussion of such questions may so discourage aspirants that they simply want to forget the whole thing; they may be sorry they ever mentioned their desire to anyone.

Because the discerning process can be so difficult, it is important for the congregation and the middle-judicatory committee to ask "Where is there support for our aspirants all along the way? Who is going to stand by them when they get discouraged or lose their way or get battered by the system?"

On a congregational level I would favor two groups: one to help the person discern the nature of the call and another to serve as a support group, standing by throughout the entire process—whether toward ordination or into an active lay role. Such a support group of three or four people could covenant to meet periodically with an individual and listen to what is happening along the way.

The strength of congregations is their ability to care about people. Do we really care about those in our midst who for whatever reasons feel something prompt them to seek a different way to serve their church?

An alternative to the congregation appointing a small support group for the aspirant would be to appoint a support person. I also look favorably on denominational systems that appoint someone from the middle-judicatory screening committee to be an advocate for the individual throughout the screening process.

Recruitment

No matter how many factors influence an aspirant in pursuing a call, the local congregation is especially qualified to evaluate potential candidates. This is where people live together and struggle with their faith over the years. Congregants observe how fellow members change and grow. They see the effects of a person's leadership efforts and how that person inspires others. They observe how he or she deals with traumas and tragedies.

If only there were training available to help congregational leaders be on the lookout for high-potential individuals. If only there were ways of helping some aspirants discern a vocation for full-time parish service as a viable option to ordained ministry. If only there were more consistent ways to plant the idea of a vocation in the church in the minds of young people.

But often a congregation's view of ministry is heavily influenced by its own experience of pastoral leadership. Gene Maeroff in his book *Sources of Inspiration* puts it succinctly.

> If religion is to be a meaningful force in today's America and if the clergy prepared by the nation's seminaries are to have any moral suasion, then more powerful voices will have to be heard....As fewer exemplars appear in the pulpits, there are fewer potential role models and it becomes ever more difficult to find people who are inspired to fill these positions in the future.[3]

Clergy role models are perceived quite differently depending on the size and location of a congregation. In the Arlin Rothauge congregational theory, you organize your thinking according to the average number of people in Sunday morning worship:

Patriarchal-Matriarchal Church	0 to 50
Pastoral Church	50 to 150
Program Church	150 to 350
Corporate Church	350 and up[4]

Each type of church demands a different kind of pastoral style, and the differences between them are both subtle and profound. For example, the difference between a Pastoral Church and a Program Church: In a Pastoral Church the spiritual needs of parishioners are met in their relationship to the pastor. In a Program Church, the spiritual needs of parishioners are met in programs, which the pastor helps plan, support, train leadership for, and coordinate. These styles are in the hard wiring of a congregation, and it is extremely difficult for a congregation to move from one size to another. Similarly, it is difficult for a cleric to move from one style to another.

Now the plot thickens. The majority of the members of mainline Protestant churches are in the two larger congregational sizes. In our seminary survey, 60 percent of the respondents came from larger churches. This seems to be a consequence of the larger numbers of people in those two categories.

But the majority of congregations in each denomination is in the two smaller categories. Two-thirds of our congregations are either Pastoral or Patriarchal-Matriarchal. This has been increasingly the case through the 1980s. The average size of an Episcopal parish dropped from 397 members in 1975 to 376 in 1985; Lutheran parishes went from an average of 518 members to 453 during the same time frame; United Methodists congregations dropped from an average of 255 to 243.[5]

At this point we need to honor the milieu out of which aspirants come as they seek ordination. At some unconscious level, church will really only be "church" when it replicates the church of one's childhood. This becomes part of our personal view of what constitutes a "good" congregation. Take aspirants who have grown up in a Program Church, give them some seminary education, and then place them in a Pastoral Church—this is like sending them to the foreign mission field without any warning about cultural adjustments.

In training programs I lead, I often encounter parish pastors who bemoan the fact that they "can't seem to get anything going in the congregation." They are talking about programs—like the ones they used to have in their home churches. Yet now they are in Pastoral Churches where their main function needs to be relating to people on a one-to-one basis. People don't need programs when they have a quality relationship with a pastor who has time to spend with them. In this size congregation, the pastor has more time to respond to the individual spiritual needs of parishioners.

For recruitment and screening strategies, the implications of the theory of congregational size are profound. Repeatedly during our interviews we heard that far more aspirants need to be recruited by and from smaller congregations because our denominations are made up mainly of those smaller units. Yet only an estimated one-third of church members belong to such congregations.

For these smaller churches, the experience of calling clergy may have been very frustrating and unfulfilling. The Presbyterian Church (USA) reports that only nine hundred of its twenty-two hundred clergy seeking calls are open to any size church. Only 12 percent of ordained ministers and candidates have expressly said they would seek a church with fewer than two hundred members.[6]

The North Indiana Conference of the United Methodist Church has 612 congregations, 376 of which have fewer than a hundred members. Another 101 congregations have memberships that range from 100 to 159. This means that toughly 78 percent of the congregations in that conference belong to the two smaller of Rothauge's categories. Yet only 42 percent of the conference's members belong to those congregations.[7]

It is no wonder that this conference instigated a grant-supported project to examine the possible use of lay pastors to serve small congregations. Sending seminary-trained personnel into some of their small rural congregations had not worked for years. The pastoral turnover was significant with the highest loss of members occurring in those smaller churches. The answer may lie in recruiting and training lay pastors who are indigenous to those areas and who can serve as bivocational clergy. A part-time person will serve as coordinator of this project.

Even with this innovative strategy, this conference has not taken the next step to intentionally recruit people who have been raised in the smaller congregations. The majority of aspirants sent to seminary by the North Indiana Conference come from its larger congregations.

There is a particular irony in this situation. Candidates with small-church backgrounds who might make ideal small-church pastors are in short supply; that means they are not available to recruit and mentor the next generation.

For laypeople in smaller, struggling congregations, there is another negative message. The Hoge-Carroll-Scheets study of the cost of ordained leadership revealed dramatically changing ratios of members to clergy.

	1965	1985
Episcopal	350 to 1	196 to 1
Lutheran	451 to 1	342 to 1
Methodist	426 to 1	247 to 1[8]

These ratios mean that a larger percentage of member contributions go to support clergy compensation and other personnel costs, rather than to cover programmatic and capital needs. Although this research inquiry confirmed strong lay support for *ordained* leadership regardless of the fiscal impact, the erosion of resources over time is bound to raise questions about the value of ordained leadership.

Because of imbalances such as these, each middle judicatory must spend more time developing a recruitment strategy and a screening process tailormade for its specific needs. It is not enough to cast a broad net for any candidates regardless of background. This would most likely exacerbate the imbalances between congregational norms and the aspirations of seminary-trained men and women.

At the end of the previous chapter, I quoted John Fletcher in his eloquent evocation of a partnership between seminary faculty and lay and clergy mentors. At a 1980 conference on "Building a Comprehensive, Collaborative Model for Training, Placement, and Sustaining Clergy," we participants experienced satisfaction from the contributions of representatives from synod, judicatory, and seminary. Only at the end of our three days together did we acknowledge that even though all of us were connected to local parishes, no participating group self-consciously represented congregations. We called for the addition of this constituency to any future conference.

That was a fine rhetorical flourish but not an idea to which many of us have subsequently devoted thoughtful consideration. With growing awareness that the "new mission frontier" is in the local parish, it is time for all of us concerned about recruitment and screening to figure out how the values and wisdom of local congregations can be factored into the process.

CHAPTER V

Middle Judicatories

In September 1989 I was asked to do a one-day consultation for the Commission on Ministry of the Diocese of Newark (Episcopal).

The contract called for a two-hour session with people wanting to explore application for postulancy in the diocese. I was told to expect eight to twelve people; I was to give them some idea of what it was like to be ordained and answer any questions. What a surprise to find thirty-eight people having signed up for the workshop.

As we started I gathered some information on the group with a differentiation exercise, having participants walk to different parts of the room based on their answers to particular questions.

Out of the thirty-eight people, twenty-six were female and twelve were male. When I asked them to divide into age categories, twenty were forty years or older. Nine were between the ages of thirty and forty. And nine were thirty or younger. Two of the men in the group were retirees, sixty or older.

When I asked how many were life-long Episcopalians, nineteen gathered at the designated side of the room; the other nineteen went to the opposite side, representing transfers from other denominations.

I then asked about their sense of call to the ordained ministry. In this differentiation, twenty-seven went to the corner indicating that they definitely felt a call from God to the ordained ministry. Six went to the corner that symbolized uncertainty and a need to explore further. Five indicated they were simply curious.

Although we were using self-evaluation, I tried to get some sense of leadership skills. Sixteen described themselves as "take charge" leaders and claimed they liked to be out in front of a group. Twenty went to the corner with the label of "consensus" or "enabling" leadership; they preferred to work behind the scenes to get things done. Two identified themselves as supporters more than leaders.

We did a quick self-rating using Myers-Briggs categories. I explained each continuum.

Extroversion	Introversion
Sensing	Intuition
Thinking	Feeling
Judging	Perceiving

The group profile was INFP—introversion, intuition, feeling, perceiving—the most mystical and questing of the twelve possible types, having a great hunger for the spiritual; "visionary" rather than "practical." My impression was that most people in this group had heard a still, small voice that they interpreted as a call to ordained ministry but which might have led them along other avenues if some spiritual direction had been available.

I left Newark with a concern that current recruitment strategies were stimulating a particular kind of person and missing those with more extroverted gifts. Was this the kind of leadership needed in this location at this time in the life of the church?

In the previous chapter I suggested that each middle judicatory propose a recruitment and screening strategy responsive to its own unique needs. I believe this is a desirable and responsible action even if that judicatory's candidates pursue other options in other locations. The discernment process should speak to the cultural values and life experiences of the people involved in the process.

When our research team set out to document recruitment and screening processes, it took us two years to make our rounds. A Board for Theological Education grant enabled us to visit fourteen Episcopal dioceses. Other support put us in touch with structures in five other denominations. As might be expected, each denomination has a different name for the committee or commission designated to oversee the candidacy processes.

Denomination	Middle-Judicatory Unit	Name of Screening Group
United Methodist	Conference	Board of Ordained Ministry
Episcopal	Diocese	Commission on Ministry/ Standing Committee
ELCA	Multisynod	Multisynodical Candidates Committee
RCA	Classis	Human Resources Committee
Presbyterian	Presbytery	Committee on Preparation for Ministry
UCC	Association	Committee on the Ministry

As we moved through twenty states, we were struck by the diversity of interests and needs of these groups. It was all too evident why all-encompassing national standards would be inappropriate. Yet we heard repeatedly how vital it was to receive clear direction and encouragement from the national level. If this were diagrammed on a flow chart, the arrows should come from above *and* from below. Those arrows should be pointing to the following areas of concern for screening committees or commissions.

Qualities for Ministry

Each time we visited a middle judicatory we observed a surprising lack of agreement on desirable qualities for ministry. The board, committee, or commission was much clearer about the characteristics they did *not* want.

Clarity about desired characteristics becomes very important as middle judicatories become proactive and actively recruit the kind of candidates they desire in the ordained ministry. It is risky to go to congregations and clergy with a request: "Find us some good candidates for ministry." Each person is going to have a personal, subjective interpretation of what "good candidate" means. It will help if committees can be quite specific about what to look for in potential recruits.

There are two potential traps in trying to get middle-judicatory decision makers to agree on desired characteristics of the ordained ministry: (1) Developing a list so long and complicated that it overwhelms congregations and clergy. To be helpful a list needs to be short and simple. I would say no more than five key characteristics. (2) Getting sidetracked by disagreements as the group tries to narrow the list to a few basic characteristics. What kind of people are needed to take the church into the twenty-first century? Images of pastoral ministry are so broad and varied these days that answering the question is bound to lead to disagreement. In spite of the pain, it is worth the effort to try to reach some consensus on this listing.

Later in this book I describe a process whereby a congregationally oriented denomination (American Baptist Churches) was able to build consensus on positive qualities for ministry among all levels of that system.

Testing the Call

Each denominational system has its own way of hearing the aspirant explain her or his call to the ordained ministry. As we indicated earlier, describing front-end-, middle-, and back-end- loading systems, several denominations hammer away early in the game at how clear the person's call is. All denominations require up front some statement of call to ordained ministry, but the United Methodist and the Episcopal systems insist on clarity before seminary training can begin.

The positive side of this emphasis is that aspirants are forced to be clear before they make major life changes—quitting jobs or selling homes. These denominations are also able to be much more supportive of their candidates once they have surmounted this initial hurdle. In our research we discovered that, even though aspirants in front-end-loading systems may chafe under scrutiny, in the long run they feel supported by the process. An overly structured process can feel much more supportive than an extremely loose one.

The United Methodists guarantee everyone they ordain a job until retirement. They must feel an acute need to monitor the progress of those to whom they extend an invitation.

A strong up-front emphasis may be instituted when there are far more people in the pipeline than can be guaranteed placement. The Educational Testing Service study compared the number of Episcopal parishes with the number of clergy since the 1950s. While parish numbers have remained stable (between seven thousand and eight thousand) over forty years, the number of clergy (active and retired) has risen from 7,500 in 1955 to 14,300 today.[1]

The downside of heavy scrutiny at the front end of the process is the anger and resentment that build up as aspirants feel compelled to repeat why they feel ordination is important to their service to the church. For some this is a depleting, cynical experience. In addition, this policy does not allow for much doubt and uncertainty. Almost one-third of the seminarians we surveyed felt it was not safe to be truly open.

At the front end of the process, the Lutheran, Presbyterian (USA), RCA, and UCC systems ask fewer questions about clarity of call and personal statements of reasons for wanting to enter the ordained ministry.

In the new Lutheran (ELCA) system, everyone is entitled to at least one year in seminary before they come under any sort of heavy scrutiny; the heavy judgment is applied in the final year of seminary, after a year of internship in a congregation and a minimum of three months Clinical Pastoral Education (CPE) training.

In the UCC at the end of seminary training, candidates must develop a statement about their pilgrimage during the in-care process and their present sense of call to ordained ministry. The statement needs to include the type of call being sought.

In the Presbyterian Church, after final ordination examinations and successful completion of CPE and field work, the candidate appears before the presbytery to make a statement of faith and give reasons for wanting ordination. Upon acceptance of that personal statement, the presbytery votes to have the person ordained.

A strong case can be made for front-end or middle- or back-end-loading ways of testing the clarity of the call, depending on the numbers of viable candidates presenting themselves in each system. I tend to favor deferring the testing of the call until later in the process because of the negative impact on recruitment of an overly stringent process prior to seminary training.

Endorsement Categories

Each of the denominations has different places where endorsement occurs and different labels for persons in various stages of endorsement.

In the United Methodist Church an individual does not attain the endorsement as a candidate for ministry until the Board of Ordained Ministry confers that label. All the testing at the district level and the congregational level and the year-long testing with a supervising pastor is simply leading up to that primary endorsement. After attaining the status of "candidate," an individual can begin seminary training.

In the Episcopal Church, one remains an aspirant until the bishop conducts an interview and designates the person a postulant. A postulant can begin seminary but must return once again to the Commission on Ministry, the Standing Committee, and the bishop to be granted the status of "candidate." This is some time after the first year of seminary. Once seminary training and ordination examinations are completed, an individual can be ordained as a deacon. Many dioceses have deacons' training programs that must be completed before one is ordained a priest.

In the ELCA there is no endorsement as a candidate until the end of the first year of seminary. The candidate status remains in place until ordination as a pastor.

In the RCA one first needs an endorsement from the local church. This simply means formal recognition and acknowledgment of intentions. After meeting with the Human Resources Committee of the Classis and being approved, the individual is considered a student-under-care. This category stands until ordination.

The Presbyterian Church first identifies a candidate as an inquirer. This requires approval by the candidate's home session, which then contacts the presbytery's Committee on Preparation for Ministry. The inquirer is asked to explore and test his or her call via interviews, reports, career counseling, or psychological evaluation.

In the UCC the first endorsement category is student-under-care. An association holds each student in this category until ordination.

Psychological Testing

It makes sense that there should be some intense psychological testing at the front end of the screening process. Being an ordained pastor means occupying a position of authority and power. Some ill-fitted people will be attracted to this career. Testing is needed to screen out those individuals.

In the RCA this step is optional, depending upon the views of the

Human Resources Committee. In the ELCA and the UCC these tests are administered while an individual is in seminary. Results become part of the information base of the seminary in its work with students.

Episcopal Church canon law states that this testing must be done prior to any individual being granted postulancy.

In the United Methodist Church, psychological exams are administered very early in the game. Once a person has made intentions known to the local pastor and the district superintendent is informed, the district superintendent appoints the aspirant a specially trained supervising pastor. One of the tasks of the supervising pastor is to hold up a mirror to the aspirant as to what issues have emerged from the psychological tests. A battery of five tests are used: Minnesota Multiphasic Personality Inventory; Strong/Campbell Interest Survey; Sentence Completion Survey; Adjective Check List; RIA (Rorschach). These tests are summarized and sent to the supervising pastor who then works with the individual for one year, dealing with the results of these surveys and the theology of the call.

A complaint we heard from aspirants and students in our research is that they never saw the results of this psychological testing or got to work with the results. Aside from the United Methodists, it did not appear to me that denominations used this material in their dialogue with aspirants and students—a missed opportunity for their personal growth and development.

Shepherds/Contacts/Advisors

Some in the church world feel that instead of testing, the most important element in recruiting and selection is a personal relationship between a student and a mature Christian who is encouraging the student toward ministry.

Among the shepherding roles in the various denominations is the supervising pastor in the United Methodist system. In the Presbyterian system an elder in the home congregation is assigned by the session. The Lutheran system appoints a contact person to develop a relationship with the potential candidate and to become his or her advocate on the Multisynodical Candidacy Committee (MSCC). Because the MSCC represents many synods, this contact person is usually from the potential candidate's home synod and can remain geographically close to the aspirant.

No system makes better use of such a person than the UCC. In many ways it is the student-in-care advisor who makes the system work. A member of the Association's Committee on the Ministry, he or she remains with the aspirant throughout the entire process. The advisor's duties are spelled out in their *Manual on Ministry*.[2] The sixteen separate functions include:

— reviewing expectations, requirements, and procedures at an initial meeting;
— insuring that the student maintains active participation in the life of a local church and association and conference activities;
— keeping in contact through letters and phone calls;
— holding at least one meeting a year to review progress, goals, and needs;
— reporting annually to the association Committee on the Ministry and the home church;
— advising the student regarding coordination of seminary courses and ordination requirements and the preparation of required materials for the association;
— providing written references;
— helping the student-in-care and the Committee on the Ministry prepare for the ecclesiastical council.

Of course the quality of such personalized assistance to any aspirant depends on the spiritual depth of the person assigned, that person's knowledge of denominational norms and policies, and the quality of the training received.

Alban's interviews with seminary students indicated mixed reactions to shepherding and mentoring functions. Overall the role of advisor or advocate was appreciated. But in systems with intense front-end scrutiny, almost anything offered was viewed with suspicion. Tragically it might be the students most in need of support who end up being the least trusting. Confident, high caliber students have few reasons to be concerned about their eventual approval. But borderline students, feeling they have been sent off with a mixed message, seem very cautious about help offered. They might view an advisor as the eyes and ears of the committee checking up on them.

It would seem more appropriate that the person assigned to an aspirant be someone not on a middle-judicatory screening committee. In most consultant training programs, one learns how important it is to be clear about who the client is and what the nature of the contract is. When someone serves as both advisor and screening committee member, it could be said that the advisor's chief client is the screening committee and not the aspirant.

A better model, given the need to provide individualized support, is for the aspirant to be the primary client—receiving help in personal and spiritual development regardless of whether the process results in ordination.

Internships, Field Work, and Clinical Pastoral Education

I tend to believe that the most critical element in the screening process is actual performance in the field. Timing of that field work is the least important factor. However, I would support encouraging, not mandating, field work prior to seminary if seminary credit could be offered. The advantage of an early experience is that it informs the student as to what she or he needs to learn.

The denominations under study vary greatly as to where and when they place requirements for some kind of field work or internship. In some Episcopal dioceses the year of internship is placed at the time prior to seminary. It becomes a key factor in determining whether or not the aspirant would be made a postulant and supported in seminary training. In other dioceses, field work runs concurrently with seminary training.

The RCA requires records of supervised ministry, internship, and CPE with written evaluation by the supervisor before a certificate of fitness is granted. This is needed for a classis to conduct ordination exams.

All ELCA seminaries require a twelve-month internship, usually between the second and third years of seminary training. Each congregation assigned an intern has an intern committee that makes a final recommendation to the seminary as to the adequacy of the seminarian's work. This internship report weighs heavily on whether or not the seminary recommends to the Multisynodical Candidacy Committee that the student be ordained.

The United Methodists place this requirement at the conclusion of seminary training, after the candidates have been ordained as deacons. After seminary, candidates have a two-year probationary period in a parish setting. Only after receiving a favorable evaluation at the end of this probationary period is someone ordained an elder. According to members of the Florida Conference Board of Ordained Ministry, each year four to six people screen themselves out of ministry during this probationary period. This probationary period tends to make the United Methodist system both a front-end- and back-end-loading system. By the time these students make it to ordination, they have learned how to work within an accountable system.

Serious discussion is now underway within the ELCA to require not only a full year of parish internship, normally between middler and senior years, but also three years of continuing education following ordination. The hope here is that candidates will come to realize that preparing for ordained ministry is a life-long task, not just a three-year stint.

As more candidates with families and economic need enter their denominational systems, there may be further adjustment of internship requirements. In a 1988 Educational Testing Service study of prospective M.Div. students, the majority reported working for wages while in college. Thirty percent reported that they had worked more than twenty hours per week. And women often were in greater need of financial aid because of the absence of a working spouse.[3]

For seminarians with families, the imposition of unpaid or low-paying internships or required field work creates a considerable hardship. The percentage of students with children rose from 25 percent in 1975 to 58 percent in 1989.[4]

Another problem is lack of mobility when one has a family. The ELCA is exploring an option that would permit second-career students to do several years of residency following ordination. This would supersede the mandated three years of continuing education.

Evaluations

An area of considerable tension between screening bodies and seminaries
is the evaluations required over an extended period of time. In an earlier
chapter I described the feelings of seminary faculty when confronted
with this mandate. Of course evaluation methods differ from one institution and denomination to another. In our interviews at four Episcopal
seminaries, we were told about three different models.

1. One seminary provides a cover letter, a faculty evaluation, and
the student's own evaluation of academic, professional, personal, and
spiritual factors. In the second year a faculty team and a field education
advisor provide evaluations and transcripts. The student completes a
self-evaluation, and there is input from the CPE supervisor. In the third
year, all of the above is again offered as well as a recommendation for
ordination.

2. Two of the seminaries use standardized evaluation forms with
very little of the kind of paperwork mentioned above.

3. One seminary relies primarily on self-evaluations prepared by
students in their second year. The evaluations are reviewed by faculty
advisors but are not changed unless there are major discrepancies. The
dean does maintain phone contact with diocesan staff to provide regular,
informal evaluations.

Regardless of method, most seminaries reported to us that evaluations were time-consuming and not necessarily worthwhile. They particularly resented having problem people passed along for whom they
were expected to be both judge and jury.

Some middle judicatories, on the other hand, perceived the seminaries as unabashed advocates who disguised questionable performance
because of the need to keep up enrollments.

This breakdown in trust is deep-seated and points to needed renegotiation of expectations. Judicatories need to respect seminaries as learning environments where people do not want to be pushed into adversarial
relationships. Seminaries need to acknowledge that they do have the
opportunity to know aspirants well—as well as anyone in the denominational system.

A relationship of trust needs to be nurtured. This will require some time and some face-to-face meetings. The United Methodists in Florida, for example, make sure that members of their Board of Ordained Ministry visit Emory, Duke, or Asbury seminaries each year to talk with their students and specific faculty members. In the Episcopal Church, some seminary faculty members participate on Commissions on Ministry. These initiatives foster workable relationships that support the best interests of candidates.

Spiritual Direction

The seminary and judicatory can work collaboratively in the critical area of the student's spiritual development. In a 1990 article on seminaries titled "The Hands That Would Shape Our Souls," Paul Wilkes reports:

> Spiritual direction has always been a staple of the Catholic seminarian's formation, but now those training to be Protestant and Jewish clerics have discovered the benefits of a continuing one-on-one relationship that focuses exclusively on this aspect of life....
>
> Southwestern, a huge Southern Baptist seminary...recently bought—at considerable cost—the entire library of a Carthusian monastery because of the thousands of volumes on Western spirituality it contained...."In the past, students came to us spiritually sound, with years of undergirding," says Southwestern's president, Russell Dilday. "Now we have students who are Christians only two months. Without spiritual formation they're going to have a rough time out there."[5]

Nevertheless, it appeared to our research team that many seminaries continue to assume that incoming students have their spiritual houses in order and that the seminary's job is to prepare students for professional ministry. Spiritual direction is not something their faculty is equipped to offer, and they often have difficulty finding budget funds to focus on this aspect of community life.

When seminaries do offer something in the area of spirituality, it is usually a course on the history and theology of spiritual formation, not directly applicable to individual spiritual direction.

This is one place where middle-judicatory screening committees can give guidance and support. It is important for committees to ask, "Where do you assume you will receive spiritual nurture and guidance while you are attending seminary?" Many aspirants should be advised to establish a relationship with a local worshipping community and a local pastor and/or a personal spiritual director.

Donald Hands and Wayne Fehr have written at length about the spiritual undernourishment they have witnessed in the patients at Saint Barnabas Center. They state the challenge clearly.

> The crucial point for the clergyperson to consider is this: Do I have a personal life and unique relationship to God? Or am I totally defined by the ministry I carry out to others? The tendency for many clergy is to take the second option. This is often bound up with an unhealthy neglect of self and a compulsive driven caretaking of others.[6]

Judicatory Workloads

This chapter has given an overview of expectations of the screening boards, committees, and commissions of the middle judicatories. Except in the ELCA and the RCA, these bodies have other responsibilities besides the screening, support, and endorsement of aspirants. These additional duties give committee members a broadened view of ordained ministry that can better equip them in the candidate-selection process. But there is a downside to the large array of duties: Screening and supporting potential clergy is a complex task and few committee members have time or energy to perform all the required functions well.

The Board of Ordained Ministry (BOM) of the United Methodist Church is likely the most overloaded of all of the middle judicatory committees. Other responsibilities assigned to the BOM of the Florida Conference included planning continuing education events for conference clergy; distribution of the ministerial education fund; planning the annual bishop's school; planning and conducting an annual retirement seminar; approving leaves of absence, including sabbatical and disability leaves; and providing for the ongoing support of clergy in the conference.

The United Methodist boards seemed to put in the longest hours, registering an average of ten hours per month, plus two full weeks in February and March when they interviewed all potential candidates, all applications for ordination, and all probationers (ordained deacons serving two years in a parish setting before gaining final approval for ordination to elder). Those serving on the executive committee of this board were putting in five to eight additional hours per month in these tasks.

Members must serve on a joint review committee, which deals with complaints against clergy. A committee on marriage, separation, and divorce must also be staffed. This committee's work is burdensome and time-consuming, for it must determine whether moral turpitude is involved, and whether the clergy in question are appointable, and report to the BOM. Still another task, determining clergy ineffectiveness, requires following four pages of procedures in the discipline that describe processes for dealing with ineffective clergy and considering exit recommendations. The only specific recruitment procedures relate to minorities.

The Commissions on Ministry of the Episcopal Church also have heavy loads that include (in addition to screening and endorsement tasks) continuing education for clergy, monitoring all vocational dioconates, and care of all ordained persons. Some tasks are unique to specific dioceses: planning annual clergy retreats, promotion of ordination among minorities, deployment of clergy; approval for canonical residences, planning vocational seminars, and a variety of tasks that bishops may assign.

Episcopal commission members reported giving an average of eight hours per month to committee work, with some dioceses demanding their presence at from one to three BACAM (Bishop's Advisory Committee on Applicants to Ministry) weekend conferences each year, at which aspirants were interviewed to become postulants. A minority of commission members reported putting in ten to fifteen hours per month, with others reporting fifteen to twenty hours per month.

The remainder of the judicatory bodies we interviewed reported an average of four to five hours per month for the disposition of their duties. Greater time commitments might be involved if one was appointed as an advisor to one or more aspirants. Earlier in this chapter I talked about the heavy workload of the student-in-care advisors in the UCC process.

Training of Judiciary Committees

Among the many activities of a screening committee, one is conspicuously absent. Our interviews indicated that only 10 percent of these bodies received any kind of training or orientation. Twenty percent of those with whom we spoke complained about lack of support. They felt their work was not highly valued by their systems. The offering of a professionally oriented training program would go far to offset that impression.

There are particular reasons why training is important. Most of the committee members we interviewed had been asked to serve a three-year term with the option of an additional term. Yet little had been offered to make the decision to serve three more years palatable. Of particular concern to these people was the adversarial role they often had to take. It was hard for them to be the bearers of negative messages that no one else seemed to want to deliver. Training in dealing with conflict and ambiguity would be extremely helpful in supporting the work of these committee members.

Professional staff need to initiate training for new people and provide back-up in monitoring the progress of aspirants. It is very difficult for a group of volunteers to monitor twenty to sixty candidates as they move through the various steps of the candidacy process. Good coaching is invaluable to make these committees and boards effective and mutually rewarding.

Conclusion

In spite of problems and defaults in the way candidacy processes are administered, screening committees, commissions, and boards work hard. Constructing procedures, discernment weekends, parish internships, and vocational testing programs takes a lot of initiative and effort.

Yet sadly, the impact of that effort will be limited to those who take the initiative to place themselves in the candidacy arena. Many with real gifts for ministry may need to be drawn out of the crowd and encouraged to consider the ordained ministry as a vocation. The challenge for these various denominational systems is to shift gears from a reactive mode and begin reaching out to recruit quality candidates.

But it is clear to me that "recruitment" as an added task of these middle-judicatory entities is impractical and unwise. The energies required for this assignment should flow from separate task forces that will not have conflicting interests. In a later chapter I will offer some models of how recruitment functions might be carried out.

CHAPTER VI

Pinch Points

Up to now this account of The Alban Institute's exploration of recruiting and screening practices has focused on four individual constituencies: seminarians, seminary faculty and staff, local congregations, and middle judicatories. I've touched on a number of problems and concerns that color these groups' perceptions of the candidacy scene.

In this chapter I would like to concentrate on three controversies: (1) the debate about oversupply versus undersupply; (2) assessing the impact of increasing numbers of female candidates; and (3) the negative image of dysfunctional clergy. These issues came up frequently in our interviews, although they are not always comfortably addressed at a national policy level. I call them "pinch points" because I believe the myths and misunderstandings surrounding these controversies contribute to a defensiveness and passivity that now characterizes the candidacy scene.

Pinch Point #1: Clergy Supply

The first controversy is about clergy supply. Are there too many candidates coming into church systems or too few? Kurtis Hess, professor of supervised ministry and director of the Office of Field Education and Placement at Union Theological Seminary in Virginia, served on the Placement System Task Force that reported to the General Assembly of the Presbyterian Church (USA) in 1992. In 1988 he spoke out about what he saw as a widely held misperception of the clergy job market.

We were told: "Hang on a little longer and the logjam will break free." We believed it. Why shouldn't we have believed it?

The conclusions of twenty years ago were probably correct based upon the data available and the assumptions held at that time. However, several significant changes occurred which altered those insights and those basic assumptions....

We in the church probably have not been as forthright about the logjam and the employment prospects with our candidates regarding their first calls and subsequent calls or lack thereof.[1]

A year later in *Presbyterian Outlook*, Carlos Wilton made this prediction.

As incredible as it may seem in a time when there are far more dossiers in circulation than vacant pulpits, there are indications that the church of the twenty-first century may not have enough ministers. Yet most of these indications are hidden by the most distinctive phenomenon to hit seminaries in the 1980s: the advent of the second-career student....The ministers ordained in the 1940s and 1950s are now retired or nearing retirement. By the year 2000, the seminary graduates of the 1960s will also be thinking about pensions and "pastor emeritus" status....By that time, today's seminary graduates will also be thinking about retirement—for they are of the same generation.[2]

What are we to make of all this contradictory information? The church world faces many paradoxes in its understanding of the issue of clergy supply. There are denominations that still have more clergy than they can place. They are the Evangelical Lutheran Church in America, the Episcopal Church, and the Presbyterian Church (USA). Denominations beginning to see a build-up of clergy waiting for placement are the United Church of Christ and the Reformed Church in America. Denominations with a serious undersupply of clergy are the Roman Catholic Church and the Church of the Brethren.

The 1987 Hoge-Carroll-Scheets study of the cost of ordained leadership documents the rise in number of ordained Protestant clergy between 1965 and 1985: 15 percent for the United Methodist Church (seeing an 11 percent decline in membership for the same period); 21 percent for the Lutheran Church in America (with a 22 percent decline in membership); 31 percent for the Episcopal Church (with a 20 percent decline in membership).

These researchers go on to cite a widely accepted rule-of-thumb: that 150 active attendees (300 members) provides financial resources and a meaningful workload for one cleric. Their national surveys demonstrated that a large number of Protestant congregations were no longer able to meet this standard.[3]

There is conflicting evidence as to where these trends will go in the future. Denominations such as the United Methodist Church claim they are going to have a serious shortage of clergy. They foresee a large number of clergy retirements within the next decade and believe they do not have nearly enough recruits in the pipeline to cover for these losses. Hoge, Carroll, and Scheets note that only eleven thousand Methodist congregations have an average of one hundred or more at worship. Yet twenty-two thousand parish pastors are guaranteed appointments.[4]

In an earlier chapter we discussed a discrepancy between the numbers of small congregations needing clergy and the numbers of seminary graduates who resist calls to congregations with fewer than two hundred members. The most recent Gallup poll information indicates that denominational fragmentation is increasing. Comparisons over the past quarter-century show all mainline groupings declining: Baptists down to 19 percent of all Americans; Methodists 10 percent; Lutherans 6 percent; Presbyterians 5 percent; Episcopalians 2 percent. Twenty-five years ago two people in three named a Protestant denomination as their religious preference. Today just over half do. This trend continues and the number of smaller congregations will grow.[5]

Difficulties in reconciling contradictory data (i.e., more retirements and clergy shortages versus smaller congregations and fewer positions) send confusing signals to those charged with encouraging aspirants. Of course differences in denominational policies influence outcomes. Also oversupply does not translate to "sorry, all jobs filled," while serious clergy shortages do not mean that "everyone is welcome."

All systems would be well advised to study the predicament of denominations where a serious imbalance of clergy to available openings has developed.

Undersupply of Clergy

A denomination with a serious shortage of clergy is the Church of the
Brethren. The denomination does not have enough quality men and
women to fulfill the variety of ministerial tasks within the church. In
October 1987 only fifty-nine pastoral profiles were in circulation for
seventy-nine listed pastoral vacancies. Among these were eight pastors
beyond retirement age and fifteen who for one reason or another were
described as difficult to place. Thus there were thirty-six viable persons
available for fifty-one positions needing qualified full-time ordained
personnel.

Each year 10 to 20 percent of both full-time and part-time place-
ments have been from outside the denomination. (In 1986 20 percent of
full-time pastors were non-Brethren.) In 1988 Bethany Theological
Seminary graduated seven candidates for pastoral ministry. Yet it was
affirmed that at least fifteen Church of the Brethren M.Div. graduates
would be needed each year.[6]

What of the Roman Catholics, another denomination with an undersupply of clergy? The Lilly-supported Educational Testing Service study
reports that in 1991 there was approximately one Roman Catholic priest
—active or retired—for every one thousand American Catholics. The
projection for the year 2000 is one priest for every four thousand.[7]

Sociologist Richard Schoenherr, an authority on clergy trends,
claims that the ranks of Catholic clergy are driven down not just by
diminishing numbers of seminarians but also by the high level of priest
resignations, and that of every ten vacancies each year only six are filled
by new ordinations.[8]

Denominations experiencing an undersupply of clergy need to come
at the task of recruitment quite differently than those still facing an over
supply. There is much we can learn from the experience of some Roman
Catholic dioceses using creative approaches. A *Washington Post* article
describes how Fr. James R. Gould, vocations director for the Diocese of
Arlington, Virginia, has raised "a bumper crop of seminarians." That
diocese has no fewer than fifty men studying for the priesthood. A sub
stantial achievement for a relatively small diocese, it also offers a ray of
hope on what is otherwise a bleak view.[9]

Much of Gould's success appears to have come through his quiet
persistence in holding up the challenge of the priesthood to whatever

group will hear him. He finds that most of his recruits are over thirty. Many are second-career people; the denomination has done much to make it easier for these people to enter seminary studies.

Reading the *Post* article, one can see that the Diocese of Arlington called one of its most committed priests to be its vocations director. Bright, committed people will be most successful in attracting people like themselves to ordained ministry.

Oversupply of Clergy

What of the denominations that still have more clergy or candidates than they can effectively place? Some denominations are seeing growing numbers of seminary graduates who are yet to be ordained and employed. As of March 1990 a Presbyterian Church (USA) study revealed that five people from the class of 1985 were still waiting; sixty-four from 1986-1988; and eighty-seven from the year 1989.[10]

I have always contended that there is never an oversupply of *effective* clergy—defining the word *effective* to mean "suiting the circumstances," not some idealized stereotype of the perfect clergyperson. The supply of clergy does not necessarily suit the circumstances of many Presbyterian congregations.

In my contact with one presbytery I perceived a system without checks and balances.

At the time of my interview twenty people were in the ordination process. Each year this judicatory added five to eight people. One committee member told me, "We rarely say no, although we sometimes make it difficult for borderline cases so they decide to drop out themselves."

I then asked the committee how many entry-level positions they had in their own presbytery.

The answer: "There are no openings. Rarely do people come back to us. This is the nature of this area."

When I asked why they continued to accept candidates, I was told, "We are accepting them for the larger church."

This policy might have been acceptable if the candidates accepted by this committee were all first-rate. But by saying yes to some borderline candidates, this committee was in effect blocking many ordained people who wanted to move but couldn't because nothing was available.

There are three negative byproducts to an oversupply situation: (1) money—the possible suppressing effect on salaries; (2) lack of mobility—clergy, especially older pastors, find it difficult to move from one parish to another and this has a demoralizing effect; and (3) lack of motivation to recruit—a diminished desire on the part of clergy to encourage people in their congregations to consider ordained ministry. Those who feel stuck where they are will be unlikely to ask anyone to enter their field.

This middle-judicatory committee reported that if the national office communicated a new policy limiting acceptances, they would emphatically support it. The Placement System Task Force of the Presbyterian Church (USA) in its 1992 proposal to the General Assembly has proposed a comprehensive strategy that should ameliorate some of the problems I saw in my visit. The document was very candid about the denomination's supply imbalance, but I am not certain that the proposal will deal with the need to define parameters. I will have more to say on that subject in my concluding comments.

Pinch Point #2: Female Candidates

The second immobilizing controversy is the dramatic infusion of so many women into clergy ranks. It is safe to say that this phenomenon has caused greater anxiety than any proposal for minority access. This anxiety is rooted in deep resistance, both conscious and unconscious, to women as ordained leaders.

In our chapter on seminarians we noted that as of 1991 30 percent of entering students were female. This was a benchmark that undoubtedly will be exceeded, although there are indicators that discouraging placement information has caused some women to have second thoughts about ordained ministry.

A good historical perspective on the acceptance of women as clergy is provided by O'Neill and Murphy in their Educational Testing Service report on seminary demographics.

From biblical times to our own, women have always been active and
influential in the ministry of church and synagogue. However, this
activity...did not gain for women a place in the hierarchy of the ordained clergy until the second half of the twentieth century. The
very few exceptions to this rule occurred in those denominations
where the power of ordination lies with the congregation. Among
Congregationalists and Disciples of Christ, for example, a few
women were ordained as early as the nineteenth century....

Between 1972 and 1987 the number of women preparing for
ordination...rose from 1,077 to 6,108, a five-fold increase (Association of Theological Schools, 1987)....These enrollment increases for
women seminarians reflect trends in higher education at large. In
1978, for the first time in American history, slightly more women
were enrolled in college than men.[11]

I have already reported that most female candidates have higher
GRE scores and demonstrate stronger academic capabilities than their
male counterparts. As fewer males have applied to seminaries, increases
in female applicants have sustained enrollment levels.

But women in most denominations are not advancing at the same
rate as men. O'Neill and Murphy cite a 1990 study by the Union of
American Hebrew Congregations (UAHC; Reform Judaism) that showed
that none of the 153 women ordained at Hebrew Union College since
1972 had become the senior rabbi in a UAHC congregation larger than
350 families.[12]

A 1990 Canadian survey reported that only half of the responding
female graduates of seminaries or theological training institutions of four
major Protestant denominations were employed in church-related positions, and of these just 16 percent were serving as a sole, senior, or co-
minister.[13]

Of interest is the growth in numbers of female Southern Baptist
ministers. Sociologist Sarah Frances Anders, who has tracked Southern
Baptist ordination statistics, says their rate of female ordinations is above
any other major denomination (although sixth in total numbers). Currently there are nine hundred Southern Baptist female clergy; in 1978
there were only seventy-eight. The significant fact is that in this denomination local congregations are autonomous and free to confer clergy status. The denomination and its conservative leadership have consistently

opposed female ordination and in 1984 passed a resolution to that effect. The resolution has seemingly had an opposite effect on local churches.

The majority of these Southern Baptist women, however, are not gaining pastoral status. Most are chaplains or are serving in mission or counseling roles. And local denominational associations have expelled some congregations that hired female ministers.[14]

The Educational Testing Service study of seminarians reports that "women are becoming doctors and lawyers at a much faster rate than they are becoming ministers, priests, and rabbis."[15]

An interesting dimension to the Canadian study of female seminary graduates was its identification of certain characteristics that these women perceived as their special strengths or gifts in ministry. These included "emphasis on affect or emotion"; "caring and nurturing"; "openness and vulnerability"; "counselling skills"; "healing ministries."[16]

Jackson Carroll, coauthor of *Women of the Cloth*, talks about the impact of women in ministry.

> We know very little about it....There are those who say women are more affirming and democratic, less authoritarian then men—and I basically agree with that—while others insist that women's ministerial style is not and should not be different from men's.[17]

Other perceptions of clergywomen raised in a number of our screening-committee interviews concerned age, marital difficulties, and possible traumatic backgrounds.

According to the O'Neill-Murphy study, the 1990 U. S. census measured a divorce-rate of 21.2 per thousand for the general population —a rate comparable to the rate for female seminarians. Age can be correlated with probability of divorce. Of those who entered seminary between ages forty-six and fifty, more than one in four were divorced. At all ages, female seminarians were more likely than male to report that they had never been married.[18]

Are female candidates (and to some degree all older candidates) held to some higher personal standard than men? It seemed from our seminary interviews with divorced women that in many cases women had come into their own at midlife and had accumulated the necessary skills in their many hours of volunteer work. They may be some of the most capable candidates the church has at this time. They have grown and appear to be different people than their younger selves who entered marriages, raised several children successfully, and became increasingly more self-confident and assertive. Spouses might not have grown nearly as fully and wanted out of marriage. By midlife these women usually held key leadership roles in their home congregations. When they felt the call to the ordained ministry and successfully received affirmation of that call, their former husbands no longer knew them as the same women they had married.

As sad as this might be, the alternative would be for these women to stifle their growth and truncate their spiritual journeys. From my perspective, these may be exactly the kind of people we need to lead the church into a promising future. We need people who have been on powerful spiritual odysseys and who have already proven themselves as capable leaders in other situations.

To be sure, there is always a mixture of types who see ordination as a desired goal. For some it will fill a psychological void. There may be those who seek ordination as a rebound to a deeply troubled personal life. And there will be still others for whom ordination is a natural culmination of a journey into service in God's church.

This is where we hope the gift of discernment is present in the lives of both women and men and in the screening committees to which they are referred. One hopes those who screen will be wise, gentle souls who enable a healthy discernment process. It should be said that those screening committees must be as wise and astute in dealing with male applicants as with female; how many males seek ordination for what are regarded as wrong reasons?

Finally, the church must be realistic about the pool available to it: This is a pool of college graduates that in 1989-1990 contained one million more women than men.[19]

Pinch Point #3: Dysfunctional Clergy

The preoccupation with dysfunction in the past lives of older female candidates is one slice of an even more pessimistic belief that the church is attracting increasingly vulnerable and endangered types of people. Some seminaries describe their students as "searchers" or "wanderers"—people who are not marching confidently into ministry directly from college.

For now these pessimistic appraisals are based on hunches rather than on hard data. (Alban's own seminary survey and interviews did not identify sufficient family and personal information to substantiate any conclusions about how background affects future performance.) People throughout the church are reacting to heightened media attention to scandals and lawsuits.

Seminary personnel reported anecdotally that front-end-loading screening processes tended to weed out the best along with the worst. Those eliminated are described as the mavericks, the self-starters, and the action-oriented types. These people tend to lose patience with minutiae and bureaucratic procedures and may, in fact, screen themselves out.

Sister Katarina Schuth, a social scientist and director of planning for the Jesuits' Weston School of Theology in Cambridge, Massachusetts, interviewed hundreds of students, teachers, and administrators in Catholic seminaries. She reports that Catholic seminarians who dropped out or were asked to leave may have included some of the brightest and most creative candidates. Acknowledging a division of opinion on how much academic quality had declined, she nevertheless found a consensus that at least "the top tenth" intellectually had been lost. She also found that those she interviewed believed that today's seminarians were more docile, dependent, academically mediocre, and less able to deal with ambiguity than those in the past.[20]

It is passive-dependent types who will endure any road block. These people have enormous patience with any procedure, whether they consider it relevant or not. Dean James Annand of Berkeley Divinity School at Yale made this point in a statement to the House of Bishops of the Episcopal Church.

> What we observe is a process that often breeds a submissive passive-aggressive attitude that undercuts the formation of the personal qualities of self-directed positive integrity that good ministry demands. Instead many of our students are either moving into passive modes of response—seeking to discern how they should try to look, think, and behave to win the necessary approval or, even more self-destructively, adopting a covertly cynical attitude about church authority....
>
> In many cases it seems that we are unwittingly producing exactly the kind of personalities that we do not wish to attract into

the ministry—passive, dependent, cynical people who learn decep-
tion, political manipulation, repressed anger, and grim persever-
ance.[21]

Some seminary faculty claim that a high percentage of students are
codependents or adult children of alcoholics. These people tend to be
high performers with an acute need to please and receive appreciation for
their performance. They are heavily into "helping"—but the kind of
helping that is often not helpful in a functioning pastorate. They need to
be needed, but they are not the kind of self-confident types required to
lead congregations into the twenty-first century.

In their book *Spiritual Wholeness for Clergy*, Donald Hands and
Wayne Fehr disclose a pattern they have encountered frequently in their
treatment of scores of troubled clergy.

> The recovery literature has identified a number of roles learned in
> dysfunctional families: the hero, the scapegoat, the clown, and lost
> child....Clergy tend to fall into two of these roles: the hero or the
> clown....The hero is almost a given role, near axiomatic, even arche-
> typal, for clergy. The hero fixes others, achieves status in the com-
> munity, and focuses energies and affect on the problems of others.
> The hero works long hours, skips vacations, or if on vacation is
> bored and restless. The hero is well trained to run away from the
> emptiness or loneliness that might be uncovered during "time off";
> it is better to keep working.[22]

Hands and Fehr describe people who have a very poorly defined
sense of personal boundaries. Many may have unrealistic expectations
of a church family substituting for the real family they lacked. Their
ideas of how to achieve intimacy may be very simplistic.

Beyond concerns about passive-dependent types and "clergy heroes," there is even greater alarm over the increasing number of highly
publicized sex scandals in the church world. Once again there are few
carefully drawn and extensive studies to document this phenomenon.
Hands and Fehr's experience with several hundred in-patients at their
clergy treatment center in Wisconsin does provide compelling evidence
that over half of those entering ministry may come from "dysfunctional
or traumatically unloving families."[23]

Lloyd Rediger, author of *Ministry and Sexuality,* believes that "approximately ten percent of clergy (mostly male) have been or are engaged in sexual malfeasance. Another fifteen percent are on the verge."[24]

Fr. Andrew Greeley's latest novel, *Fall from Grace*, builds a fictional case study of pedophilia in the Roman Catholic Church. In interviews Greeley estimates that more than two thousand priests may have committed such crimes during the past twenty-five years.[25]

There are, however, more cautious voices. David Hardy, general counsel for ELCA, says: "There's no greater incidence of clergy sexual abuse today than in the past. What we're dealing with is victims who are more willing to come forward and a backlog of cases."[26]

How does all this negative and confusing information influence feelings about the kinds of people needed in ministry? In this controversial area, as well as in the areas of clergy supply and female candidacy, misinformation and misperceptions cause us to think reactively. There is plenty of gossip but almost a dread of dialogue. Right now in many denominations there is a great deal of improvisation at the local level trying to deal with perceived problems. That means, in most cases, a hunkering-down mentality that limits people's vision about possibilities.

There will always be a need for strong, effective screening processes. The parish ministry is going to attract some of the wrong kinds of people. The role of parish pastor still holds enough honor, esteem, and authority among the faithful that it will attract those whose egos need massaging. The clergy role is also one that interacts with people when they are most vulnerable. As such it will attract potential abusers and addictive or codependent types.

But even though it is prudent to look for the "baggage" a candidate brings into the process, we must not go overboard. I constantly meet effective clergy who tell me: "If I had to go through our denomination's screening process today, I would never make it into ordained ministry."

For those denominations using heavy front-end-loading screening procedures, it may be time to say "well done" and move into a different mode. This radical shift is what challenges us today. We are still in a passive state and are not defining the kinds of people needed. We are not casting our nets widely enough.

James Annand puts it this way.

We seek to intersect this problem by turning the psychology around. We suggest shifting the thrust of screening to a much more intentionally identified recruitment mode, stating at the outset that the church affirms all calls to ministry. There will be no need to prove something missing in personal make-up that will occasion "rejection." We can then take a more apostolic position that the church is seeking a few persons to enlist for special ordained purposes. It is not a rejection of many but the enlistment of a few."[27]

Conclusion

This chapter has highlighted three "hot buttons" of the church world: clergy supply, female candidates, and clergy dysfunction and malfeasance. I have chosen to address these issues in this way because I believe they are immobilizing us at a critical time of need. That need is to attract and stimulate the kinds of people who are able to nurture and sustain local congregations to help them come alive and grow as communities of faith.

All three "pinch points" require renegotiation of expectations around well-documented, well-disseminated facts. There must be much more careful monitoring of the applicant pools of each denomination. Then that data can be applied proactively to the design of recruitment strategies in which committed stakeholders at *all* levels of the church play key roles.

In 1980 John Fletcher's analysis of the future of seminaries in this country communicated the urgency of today's situation.

In an era of increasingly fragmented seminary life and part-time attendance, opportunities for serious self-knowledge and mutual reflection on the student's ethical, educational, and emotional background will be markedly fewer....The likely result is that more untested and problematic persons will enter the ministries of denominations already affected by de-professionalization. The laity who receive these thinly prepared graduates...will despair even more. Will they be motivated to reach even deeper into frayed pockets to support seminaries?[28]

CHAPTER VII

Responding Across Boundaries

The previous chapter talked about confusion and controversy over issues that should be rousing us to action but instead may be perversely immobilizing us. Yet I must say that as I traveled around the country doing interviews for our candidacy study, I found plenty of passion for change. This letter following up a Commission on Ministry survey is typical.

> There is no national strategy...regarding the needs of and for the ordained ministry. The boards so charged are each focused on their turf and have not picked up the need to have a truly churchwide focus....If we are serious about a churchwide strategy, it will have to be a full commitment at all levels....I ask that we stop rearranging the deck chairs on the Titanic and rechart our course.

The writer of this letter went on to spell out a half-dozen initiatives that needed to occur in his denomination. He acknowledged that there can be no simplistic solutions to the current difficulties the church is having recruiting and screening the best for parish ministry. The solutions chosen need to be wholistic or they will fail. For example:

> It is difficult to ask clergy to recruit the best candidates for ministry without first being clear about what characteristics they should look for.

> It is unwise to begin a recruitment program without first becoming clear about the mission of the church.

> It makes no sense to develop a clear mission without first checking with a wide array of people within a system.

It will be dangerous to seek highly qualified candidates if their seminary education does not challenge them.

It will be hard to enhance seminary programs without more money, and raising that money will be difficult without dealing head-on with the disenchantment some clergy and laity feel toward seminaries.

It will be imprudent to ask clergy to recruit the best until they can be confident that the screening committees of their denominations won't embarrass them with extremely arduous and humiliating screening processes.

It will be problematic to ask screening committees to become more user-friendly without first convincing the church that this is crucial.

It makes no sense to go after the brightest and best candidates for ministry without first assuring them that the church will be there for them when they're looking for placement.

In short the church needs a complete strategy for getting at the current malaise—a strategy that deals with the change systemically and systemwide. It is going to require vision and courage to do this. I am confident that this kind of leadership can be mustered in mainline denominations. What is needed first is a comprehensive picture of how each of the separate parts could contribute to the whole. The following are some examples of initiates that The Alban Institute has identified in our exploration of recruitment and screening policies and procedures.

National Initiatives

Six recruiting and screening functions seem most appropriately placed with those who are staffing and serving on national bodies: forecasting trends, stimulating dialogue, policy making, developing evaluative instruments, designing instructional and orientation materials, and training regional consultants.

Forecasting

National offices are best able to study trends within a denomination, forecasting personnel needs for the next decade based on realistic assessments of congregational needs and resources. College enrollment figures, census data about population changes, and such studies as the Hoge-Carroll-Scheets study about the economics of ministry are readily available and may in fact be currently available in denominational databases.[1] But how to share this information throughout a system? A positive example is the *Bits and Pieces* newsletter put out regularly by the Study to Enrich Inquirers and Candidates (SEIC) project of the Presbyterian Church (USA). These abstracts contain a great deal of honesty. The newsletter lists as its purpose.

> To collect a variety of observations on church vocations
> To share some Presbyterian Church (USA) vocational data
> To invite persons to weigh the realities of church openings
> To help persons plan their professional development.[2]

Stimulating Dialogue

In 1988 the American Baptist churches in the USA used a Lilly Endowment grant to support an effort to develop a list of positive qualities for ministry. They were aware of the difficulties inherent in forging a consensus in a congregationally oriented denomination; they acknowledged that given the autonomy of local congregations, they needed to carry out a wide consultation. The Educational Ministries Office invited leaders from all sectors of American Baptist Churches to a two-day consultation on the qualities that should be listed. Participants immediately recognized that hard choices needed to be made.

Their answer was to develop three lists that identified desired characteristics at different age levels (youth; traditional college age; second career). It is one thing—an ideal—to think about desired qualities in a fully mature, developed, and effective pastor. But this group chose to frame these qualities in the present tense as stages of development in a changing and growing person. A summary of this project appears in Appendix II.

More recently the Presbyterian SEIC project has developed its own inventory of "Primary Qualities for Persons in Professional Ministry." At a series of gatherings over a three-year period, participants, including seekers, inquirers, members of Committees on Preparation for Ministry, and representatives of theological institutions, have been communicating (a primary objective is enhancing partnerships between presbyteries and theological institutions) and generating a rich array of research data.[3]

Policy Making

At the national level policies need to be set that will guide middle-judicatory screening committees. My previous example from a visit to a presbytery shows how helpful guidelines would have been in that situation. Nationwide policy is especially needed to inform the process of discernment by middle-level screening bodies.

A primary obstacle to policy making is the fear of reinforcing negative stereotypes and setting quotas. This leads to inaction and passivity. If there is to be any breakthrough, "it is the responsibility of leadership to lead." Those are the words of the Recruitment and Screening Committee of the Board for Theological Education of the Episcopal Church when it issued its report in 1990 and called upon its House of Bishops to help "define the shape of the ministry of the church in light of the Mission Imperatives and the Decade of Evangelism."[4]

Developing Evaluative Instruments

National examinations remain controversial within the denominations using them. Seminaries claim that they interrupt the final year of seminary life. No one is ordained in the Presbyterian or Episcopal systems without passing some kind of exam. A great deal of energy goes into preparation; this may detract from other studies. Students may select a seminary based on that institution's record of helping with these exams.

In the ELCA an "approval essay" is required. The essay is in response to questions developed by an ad hoc committee assembled by the Division for Ministry at the national level. Both the seminary and the Multisynodical Candidates Committee get to read the essay and make recommendations based on its contents.

(The RCA, the UCC, and the Methodist Church do not require national examinations.)

These kinds of examinations follow an academic model for training clergy. Certainly high value should be placed on an educated clergy. But care must be taken not to communicate an incorrect message: that if you can pass one of these comprehensive exams, you are equipped to be a competent pastor. Nothing could be further from the truth.

I do not have a specific initiative to offer as an example, but in my conversations during our interviews I did receive a number of suggestions including:

— using less ponderous and threatening examination formats;

— using the exam as only one factor in determining suitability for parish ministry;

— including on exam students' comprehension of complexities of pastoral role.

— giving the exam before the final semester of seminary so feedback can inform the remaining months of education.

Designing Instructional Materials

Because the development of instructional audio-visual materials is quite expensive, this task is most appropriately placed at the national level. It was suggested that congregations would benefit in their individualized contacts with prospective candidates if they could see a video on images of ordained ministry. This is a job for professionals but is well worth the cost.

Training Regional Consultants

National church offices could also train consultants who would function at the regional level to work with middle-judicatory task forces on recruitment strategies.

Let's now turn our attention to the recruitment and screening role of regional entities.

Regional Initiatives

A number of denominations have four administrative levels, each with its own set of tasks. The top level is the national organization and the bottom is the local congregation. That leaves two intermediate levels. Here are some examples, with the larger, regional entity listed first.

Presbyterians	synods and presbyteries
Lutherans	regions and synods
Episcopalians	provinces and dioceses
Methodists	conferences and districts
UCC	conferences and areas

In our experience at Alban, one of those levels generally has less clout. In the Presbyterian Church, for example, presbyteries are regarded as the emerging power. In the Methodist Church, on the other hand, bishops preside at the conference level with district superintendents functioning in subordinate positions.

From our review of recruitment and screening needs, I would say that training and consultation functions are most effectively performed at the regional level.

Regional Consultants

This role addresses difficult issues arising in either recruitment or screening. If denominations are to be proactive about recruitment developmental strategies are in order. It is more cost-effective to work with a cluster of middle judicatories communicating about the kinds of resources available and successful efforts in other parts of the country than for each middle judicatory to work independently.

An example of a recruitment strategy carried out regionally is the "Assessment and Leadership Opportunity Event" model offered in the Presbyterian Church (USA) "Call System Proposal."[5] Such events would be offered to people at the very beginning of the process and would be used to complete a profile based on self-reflection, testing, and interviews.

As a result of our research study, I have developed strong convictions about the need for each middle judicatory to appoint two committees: one for screening tasks, the other for recruitment activities. Even though these two groups would need to work hand-in-hand, some delineation of responsibilities needs to be mediated by a regional consultant. It is reasonable to anticipate certain exceptions from standard screening for certain appealing aspirants. These exceptions need to be negotiated in advance; an example might be capable minority candidates who might become discouraged in a drawn-out front-end-loaded process. (Doubtless minority participation should be sought for a recruitment task force.)

Regional Trainers

Less than 20 percent of the individuals we interviewed on various denominational bodies reported having any training for their screening or recruitment tasks. This was one of the most troublesome findings from our field work. Turnover was fairly high on these committees; training of new people was spotty.

I was surprised that newly appointed members did not insist on training. Yet these people probably assumed that as long-time active members in their churches, they would be able to recognize a potentially good pastor. Most were unaware of the conflict that lies ahead. Coming to conclusions on candidates who obviously have good potential is rewarding. Resolving dilemmas about those who seem to be unsuited for ministry is uncomfortable but manageable. It is when confronted with someone who sits in the middle—neither superior or inferior—that many screening committee members feel at a loss. Here clergy have an easier time with discernment than laity. Clergy tend to be less naive about the nature of the call to ordained ministry. Many have watched as their colleagues dropped out of ministry because they had no clear discernment process to begin with.

For those appointed to screening committees, a quality training program is needed to deal with questions such as "What is a call?" "What is ordination?" Scriptural study on the gift of discernment would be helpful. Understanding the concept of "tough love" would be especially valuable.

Training in conflict resolution would be another important ingredient in any regionally directed orientation for screening committees. It is important to have diversity of opinion on any committee. The quality of decision making is going to be higher when resolution can be gained from strongly held points of view. But this will not happen if committee members have no preparation for conflict situations.

Seminary Initiatives

Seminaries are pivotal, of course, and their roles and responsibilities may be very broad and all-encompassing depending on their denominational ties. As I noted earlier, in some middle-loading denominations these institutions are the primary facilitators of the candidacy process. Their insights are the foundation for decision making.

During our interviews and our seminary research conferences, I was impressed by several suggestions that could serve as models for how theological institutions contribute to a comprehensive multilevel candidacy strategy.

Coaching Lay Internship Committees

All the denominations in our study emphasize at least three months of Clinical Pastoral Education (CPE) as a requirement or strong recommendation for ordination. Seminary faculty reported their concern that local committees relied on the CPE experience to repair dysfunctional behaviors. Insufficient and inaccurate feedback could damage a person irreparably.

Would it not be healthier, I was asked, if seminaries worked cooperatively with lay internship committees to develop ways to get more accurate feedback? That kind of coaching would better equip the local bodies to do a fair and comprehensive assessment of candidates' potential.

Appointing field-work directors at the seminary level and ensuring them reasonable workloads would mean those directors could organize the assessment process, supervise the experience, and share in evaluations with lay committees. They would also have the time to debrief students, an important function as people do not learn simply from an experience. They learn from disciplined reflection on an experience.

Evening and Other Part-Time Study

There are some clear advantages and disadvantages to part-time seminary attendance. It is unlikely that part-timers will experience the full life of seminary communities. Getting them into field-work assignments may also present some difficulties if they need to continue their full-time employment. I suspect the greatest obstacle is from the seminaries, which find it difficult to provide flexible class periods or offer an entire M.Div. curriculum via evening classes.

On the plus side, we would have graduates with the skills to earn a living in some vocation other than parish ministry. As I look into the future of congregational life, I feel that in the next decade from one-third to one-half of our churches will be moving from full-time pastorates to part-time ministry. As we know, the majority of mainline congregations are small. When they cross the line between full-time and part-time, they are going to prefer a pastor of their own (not shared with another parish) who will serve them part-time. This means people are needed who are accustomed to flexible lifestyles and who have the gift of moving from one focus to another.

The other strong plus for inviting working people to attend seminary part-time (particularly in the evenings) is that this will bring more ethnically and economically diverse people into systems. Seminary is no longer the privileged opportunity for well-to-do majority people. And there need to be ways to make it possible for students to avoid monumental debt.

A final advantage to part-time programs is to give laypeople the opportunity for in-depth biblical and theological learnings even if they do not intend to apply for holy orders.

Seminary-University Networks

One possible new alliance would be between seminaries and universities or colleges where potential ordination candidates would receive seminary credits for courses offered in university or college religion departments.

Claremont School of Theology and San Diego State University are trying out such an arrangement. I understand that ten San Diego State students enrolled in this program, and five later enrolled at Claremont where they maintained strong grade point averages. Claremont would like to expand this program to other educational institutions.

These seminary-university networks could be facilitated by college chaplains who may be aware of students with the greatest potential for effective ministry.

Middle-Judicatory Initiatives

Developing a Vision

Leadership at this level is crucial. The executive or bishop needs to engage the system in developing a vision that matches the needs of the area for the next ten years. Our interviews revealed that most screening committees were carrying out their work with little or no direction from their judicatories. They were almost surprised when asked questions about the kind of directives they received. In their responses they seemed to be saying, "Well, everyone here knows what we are looking for."

The result could be an overpersonalization of qualities needed for tomorrow's clergy. Most screening committees we studied had not tried to gain consensus on characteristics desired or needed. Such a dialogue should grow out of the mission needs of the local area. Without such clarity, it is almost impossible to develop a clergy profile. Too often church executives' characterizations of competent clergy models do not reflect a long-term strategy.

I recall working with one denomination trying to piece together a recruitment effort. We suggested that the bishop drop by for a few minutes to give his input. After a few minutes of social conversation, I asked him for any suggestions he could make about the type of clergy we should be looking for. A blank look came over his face. The silence was deafening as we waited for his response. He finally cleared his throat and said, "Well, try to get ones with strong faith."

When I asked the same question of a younger, more recently elected church executive, I got another vague answer. He was in touch with the drawbacks of the local screening process. He was concerned about high turnover of committee members and the fact that they had received little training. But as to a recruitment strategy for his judicatory for the next ten years, he had not given it any thought.

In my concluding comments, I will deal with the difficulty many people in the church have with the word *recruitment*.

Vocational Testing

Arguments over how and when to test the validity of a call continue to trouble conscientious people working to improve candidacy processes. I am concerned when I have priests tell me that they would discourage any parishioners showing an interest in ordained ministry. Their reason is that they want to spare them the stress of enduring all the obstacles placed in their paths.

Yet I believe there should be testing processes in place for those who are unsure of their call and want help in making that decision. I visited the Diocese of Atlanta and was impressed by their Vocational Testing Program (VTP). This is a six- to nine-month program in which an aspirant is placed in a parish setting under the supervision and tutelage of its rector. The rector is responsible for seeing that the aspirant has a variety of experiences in ministry, including urban and institutional settings. A lay committee as well as a diocesan peer group provide opportunities for reflection.

All this is managed while the aspirant is working full-time in a secular job. So people who would find it economically risky to commit to candidacy have an opportunity to test their skills in ministry and find out whether this is a true calling. I have some question about whether the program should be required, as it is now, or optional. It seems to me that this kind of process must be individualized.

I want to share concerns expressed by Bishop Frank Allan in Atlanta, as he reflected on the work of his Commission on Ministry and the diocese's VTP. Bishop Allan's frustration with the system was that although it is probably one of the most highly sophisticated programs for screening aspirants in the country, some specific needs were not being met. Several rural parishes needed priests who were not aiming for large parishes and would be content to serve country parishes faithfully and well. The VTP was not producing that type of clergyperson. And not one minority person had progressed through the program.

Bishop Allan believed that the VTP had been an effective tool to deal with the onslaught of those who have presented themselves each year. In many cases their calls needed to be questioned. But the VTP was not an effective tool for identifying and bringing forward those who could match the bishop's targets of special need.

Vocation Days

I first heard about this recruitment thrust from Alban consultant Ed White, who interviewed personnel within the Diocese of Texas. This judicatory conducts a day of vocational exploration every two years. The original purpose was to encourage younger people to consider full-time service in the church. (Among women and men in Episcopal seminaries, only one in five is under age thirty.)[6] Even though this intent is not being fulfilled, the Commission on Ministry feels the vocation days are useful for other reasons.

Every two years the chair of the Commission on Ministry invites all clergy to send to the bishop names of persons they feel would make good priests. Some specific qualities and characteristics are suggested. The bishop then sends a personal letter inviting these people to the vocational conference. The commission intentionally does not send out blanket invitations to the diocese, and people already in the process are not included.

In 1992, thirty-five people attended. A wide array of presenters included the bishop, a commission member, and someone from a specialized ministry such as chaplaincy. The importance of lay ministry was stressed. The last item on the agenda was an explanation of the steps to be taken to be accepted as a postulant and then as a candidate.

A variation on this approach is used in the Roman Catholic Diocese of Chicago, which regularly holds an event called "Weekend with

Clergy." People wanting to explore a vocation in the priesthood are invited to spend some informal time with parish clergy. A professionally produced videotape on images for ordained ministry is shown. Such videos are now being produced by the Roman Catholic Diocese of Saginaw (Michigan) and the Division for Ministry of the ELCA.

College Chaplains

Back in the 1950s and 1960s, spotting quality candidates for the ordained ministry used to be part of a college chaplain's job description. Since then several things have happened to discourage that effort. The first was the oversupply of aspirants in a number of denominations. The other was a major shift in the role of the college chaplain, along with significant budget cuts.

The time seems ripe for middle judicatories to once again engage with college chaplains. There could be a conference around recruitment with significant time devoted to a discussion of the qualities needed for effective ministry. Chaplains should be briefed on screening practices, ways to follow up with people expressing interest, and a specific feedback mechanism for chaplains. They need opportunities to express any negative feelings they have about a recruitment role.

Religion Departments

Shortly after World War II, American colleges and universities began treating the study of religion as one of the new frontiers in teaching and scholarship. For the most part denominational and seminary leaders applauded this phenomenon. As mentioned earlier in this chapter, there is a renewed interest on the part of seminaries in partnerships with universities and colleges.

Paradoxically while religion departments have attracted the interest of many students, those same students do not seem to be motivated to consider parish ministry as a vocation. Why shouldn't middle judicatories engage with these students and see whether their genuine curiosity about religious questions translates into a call to ordained ministry?

The Educational Testing Service study of M.Div. candidates documented that 21 percent of its total sample had majored in religion or theology and that this field of study was far more common among men (24 percent) than among women (15 percent).[7] This finding might suggest a way of identifying more male candidates.

Recruitment Outreach

Recently I had an opportunity to follow up on some of the outreach strategies that surfaced during our study. The state of Wisconsin attracted my attention because it has three distinct Lutheran denominations (Evangelical Lutheran Church in America, Lutheran Church-Missouri Synod, and the Wisconsin Evangelical Lutheran Synod). All three subscribe to the Lutheran confessions, but to compare the three would be like comparing Presbyterians with Southern Baptists with Nazarenes.

BecauseI knew that all three were concerned about the need for active recruitment of candidates for the ordained ministry, I worked with them to secure a grant from the Siebert Foundation. Each body agreed to form its own recruitment task force with which I would work over the course of eighteen months.

In phase 1 we would critique current recruitment methods. Based on our assessment, we would create some alternatives. Phase 2 would involve experimentation with these alternatives over a one-year period. Phase 3 would engage each denomination in an evaluation.

This project is still underway, but already there are some indicators of problems and opportunities. The project has shown how difficult it is to begin a recruitment initiative when most people perceive an oversupply of clergy. The Milwaukee ELCA Synod in a metropolitan region usually has more clergy trying to get in than they can use. One reason is its openness to women and second-career people.

On the other hand, the Lutheran Church-Missouri Synod has faced a shortage of seminarians primarily because it is not admitting women into its ordination track. The Wisconsin Synod has experienced shortages of seminarians for the same reason and also because until this year it has not admitted second-career students.

Another insight is the fact that clergy in long pastorates have a clear advantage in their recruiting efforts. They have lived with the families of their congregations for a decade or more; they are much more knowledgeable about the quality of family life surrounding their young people than a new pastor would be.

I prompted all three church bodies to see if each group could agree on five basic qualities to look for in aspirants. Surprisingly task force members assumed that such qualities were so obvious that they didn't merit discussion. They believed they would recognize a superior candidate when they saw one. Furthermore, none of the executives involved had provided a sense of their systems' needs to the screening committees. This left committee members operating with their own very personalized notions.

For a more detailed account of this study, see Appendix III.

Congregational Initiatives

In 1990 Bishop Darold Beekmann of the Southwestrn Minnesota Synod of the ELCA observed that as laity gained more influence in the church, the pastor's role and influence had diminished. He remembered his seminary days in the 1950s. He knew he wouldn't get rich as a pastor, but he was encouraged by his pastor and that made a difference. In today's church world, he says, Lutherans want very educated leaders, but "they couldn't think of encouraging their own kids within the congregation to consider the ministry."[8]

Yet laity are highly motivated to seek first-class ordained leadership for their own congregations. This was substantiated through the research study reported in the book *Patterns of Parish Leadership.*[9] The authors described what Loren Mead calls "a turning-point dilemma." The economic basis for full-time ordained leadership in a majority of Protestant churches no longer exists. But the ordinary church member steadfastly refuses to accept leadership alternatives.

How does this contradiction affect the way local congregations think about their own members as prospective ordained clergy? Bishop Beekmann sees the situation negatively. It is my hope that with guidance and training from middle judicatories (and with the use of educational resources produced at the national level) people at the parish level can be transformed into stakeholders in the task of undergirding ordained ministry because, in the end, their congregations will benefit. In expressing that hope I am fully aware of the current trends toward localism and parochialism. I want to propose some promising ideas that have been shared with me during this candidacy study.

Parish Identifiers

This model selects one or two key lay leaders within congregations to act
as "identifiers" of potentially effective parish clergy. Because clergy are
often busy with much on their minds, the idea here is to turn over the
task of recruitment to a gifted layperson who feels some personal sense
of call to this ministry.

Possibly these people should function as "silent recruiters." Few
would know that such a function was being carried out. This might have
more impact on those being recruited—being singled out by a layperson
and asked to consider a clerical vocation.

Imagine also such laypeople tracking aspirants through college and
seminary, spending time with them on vacation breaks and taking an
interest in school progress. Throughout all the trials and tribulations in
preparation for ordained ministry, these aspirants would know that someone at home was supporting them and praying for them.

It is my understanding that in the Presbyterian Church (USA), elders
are appointed for this purpose and that a number receive training from
their presbyteries.

Vocations Seminars

A United Methodist colleague of mine, Richard Haid, claims that most
people spend more time planning their vacations than they do their careers. He feels that every congregation should consider offering career-
center activities to their members as a way of assisting people find more
meaning in their daily lives. Richard was formerly a CEO of an insur-
ance company but now works full-time as a consultant on vocation initiatives.

Related to this concept is the work of Jackie McMakin and Sonja
Dyer, who manage what they call "Lay Labs." These weekend seminars
or series of weeknight workshops offer laypeople the opportunity to discover their call to ministry—not the ordained ministry but the ministry of
the baptized. The central thesis is that everyone has a call from God to
do something specific with their life, but most ignore or avoid the call.
Their book *Working from the Heart* describes how this process operates.[10]

Any congregation offering programs such as those Haid or

McMakin and Dyer suggest will find that members appreciate the chance to bring clarity to their life's work. As congregations foster this kind of reflection, the outcome can be more recruits for either lay or ordained service.

College-Student Parish Internships

A common testimony from older pastors is the importance to their call of an opportunity in college to test themselves in church ministry. The experience of preaching, teaching, and performing a leadership role was influential in selecting ministry over other careers.

Today's college-age youth experience fewer ministry opportunities. The fast-paced life in high school and college seems to discourage parish involvement. Yet most congregations will affirm their strong commitment to youth.

This initiative is a return to the old model of student involvement. It must be well thought out and structured to provide intense and close-range exposure to the primary facets of parish ministry over sufficient time to allow for both hands-on experience and disciplined reflection. It should be done cooperatively with other congregations, so that students do not work in their own churches. (A middle judicatory could help orchestrate this cooperation.) Conceivably these internships could be offered as a part-time opportunity, allowing students to earn money in summer jobs. Both high school and college students should be considered.

Something similar is being tested at Princeton Theological Seminary. In this program participants spend ten to twelve days as observing, inquiring interns, shadowing ministers in their tasks. An internship is capped off with four days of reflection, workshops, and worship at the seminary. College chaplains and parish clergy nominate people for this experience. They then receive a personal invitation from the seminary.

Training of Selected Clergy

Not all clergy are good at identifying people with high potential, nor are they particularly effective at getting them to consider ordained ministry. Growing out of a specific middle-judicatory strategy, clergy with particular gifts and background might be invited into a special training program.

Such gifted people will be most likely to attract others with special attributes.

The training would concentrate primarily on how to identify those who appear to have the appropriate prerequisites. Consideration needs to begin with a consensus listing of characteristics desired by that middle judicatory. Then trainees need help learning how to interact with prospective applicants.

The Archdiocese of Saint Paul and Minneapolis is experimenting with Leadership Interview Training Workshops in which five priests from each deanery participate. Once trained, these priests are given opportunities to use their skills interviewing actual candidates.

In addition to developing connecting skills, these clergy could also be offered some ideas of how to engage these people in certain parish activities—to give them a taste of the leadership role and to give the mentors a chance to observe them. Prospective applicants could be nurtured in a variety of roles to see how fulfilled they are in lay ministries. I am not sure I would be in ministry today if I hadn't been given opportunities in Luther League, the choir, and preaching at youth services.

Conclusion

In this chapter I have given some examples of how all constituencies can refresh and renew the church's challenge to people whose aspirations now take them into other professions at twice and three times the rate of ordained ministry.

At the completion of our exploration of candidacy processes in several denominations, I have an even stronger conviction that the development of overarching visions and strategies is desperately needed at this point in church history. All levels in the system must participate, but national leadership must set the tone, and the focal point must be the middle judicatory.

Finally, for this kind of collaborative effort the finger pointing of the past must give way to renegotiating relationships and developing values that can be held in common. One of the participants in a seminary conference wrote me afterwards to say from her heart, "For me as a former candidate, a Candidates Committee chair, an exam-reader, and now seminary staff, the need for continuing and supportive communication throughout the system is critical!"

CHAPTER VIII

My Personal Convictions

These are times of great uncertainty and conflicting perceptions within mainline denominations. Many feel that membership losses have hit bottom over the past decade and may be reversing. Yet in the past three years denominations have experienced serious budget shortfalls, making it less likely that major new initiatives can take place in the church world. At the same time confidence in clergy seems to be eroding.

The current problems denominations are having in recruiting the brightest and best candidates for ordained ministry have much to do with these negative impressions. I have been particularly struck by the low numbers of college students who view the church as a vehicle for social change in the world.

When the church is regarded as a nice establishment that is irrelevant to the important issues of our age, we should not be surprised that we are having difficulty attracting the special kinds of people needed to lead today's congregations.

In the last ten years we seem to have lost our way. Within that decade there has been no religious leader with major impact on our culture. I am talking about the impact of people such as Gandhi, Martin Luther King, Jr., William Sloan Coffin, Paul Tillich, Eugene Carson Blake, and Richard and Reinhold Niebuhr. Maybe there are few heroes in any profession today. But when was the last time you saw a TV program in which the local parish priest was the hero who saved the day?

I have felt that the vocation of ordained clergy may be getting an overload of people with deep emotional and psychological problems. An earlier chapter dealt with some educated guesses on this subject. If those guesses are on the mark, it may be that the attraction is the sense of the church as a respectable parental institution that cares for people. Ordination represents a guarantee that the church will "be there" for a lifetime. But during that lifetime many other people can be damaged by the cleric who uses authority inappropriately.

Yet, as concerned as we are about unsuitable candidates, we seem to be increasingly reluctant to expect people of unusual talent to make the sacrifices necessary for ordination. Although the seminarians in our survey said their parents had encouraged them, there is considerable evidence that families feel it is no longer an honor to have a son or a daughter enter this field.

What is missing in the image we present is passion and urgency. We seem unable to convey a sense of how a biblical witness can still be the conscience of a nation. Have we forgotten the importance of a prophetic witness in the face of the many social injustices of our day? Have we forsaken the importance of sound theological reflection as a key component to right living? Have we backed away from the idea of lay ministry as a transforming agent in a broken and hurting world?

I am certain there is still much passion or urgency in our congregations and in the citizenry at large. I still encounter people who are outraged that 40 percent of those in prisons in our country are of Afro-American descent and that the U.S. puts more people behind bars than any other nation in the world. Caring people are angry that the wealthiest nation in the world has millions of people who are homeless. A higher percentage of people get their daily bread from soup kitchens than did so in the Great Depression. The gap between the rich and the poor continues to widen.

No wonder people take drugs. They live in hopelessness, failing to see meaning in their lives, needing to escape the daily realities of their lives. Their physical and spiritual needs are sorely neglected. The word spiritual is paramount.

With all the problems this nation has, we continue to place the church outside the mainstream, almost voiceless in the midst of intolerable human need.

There is a growing cynicism in the political process, and this affects the way our church leaders perceive their own influence. Thus they compromise their positions at moments when the church could let its light shine. Items:

— A panel of U. S. Roman Catholic bishops calls sexism "a moral and social evil" (*Washington Post,* April 10, 1992) but affirms the church's ban on ordaining women.

— As Protestants the majority of us affirm the ordination of women, acknowledging their academic and social capacities, but resist turning over our larger congregations to their leadership.

— A denomination states that gay or lesbian lifestyles should not be considered an aberration of God's natural order but concludes that ordination of a gay or lesbian is out of the question.

— As a church we continually affirm multiculturalism, heterogeneity, and the equality of all persons under God, yet our Sunday morning worship hour is the most segregated time in our nation.

And we wonder why people of talent and vision may not feel challenged to consider ordained ministry as a career option?

A study by the Search Institute provides a discouraging picture of the effectiveness of the traditional denominations in producing mature disciples. In six major denominations less than one-third of a sample of eleven thousand had an "integrated faith" (i.e., faith that integrates a vertical relationship with God with a horizontal ministry to fellow human beings). Here are a few of the specific findings.

— 66 percent never or rarely encouraged someone to believe in Jesus Christ;
— 42 percent never or rarely talked about the work of God in their lives;
— 72 percent never marched, met, or gathered with others to promote social change;
— 57 percent did not engage in daily prayer;
— 66 percent did not read the Bible;
— 52 percent never donated time to help the poor.[1]

Quite possibly, the recruitment problems of mainline denominations relate to the lukewarm religiosity that marks the past ten years. We are reaping what we have sown.

Several years ago Lee Iacocca, former CEO of the Chrysler Corpo-
ration, was reflecting with reporters about the fact that the automobile
industry here in America fell asleep at the switch during the 1970s and
1980s; Japanese automobiles took over the American market simply by
producing better quality cars. Now we are hearing that once again
American-made automobiles can outsell foreign models.

In a similar fashion we in mainline denominations may have fallen
asleep at the switch. Think of how different our clergy recruitment tasks
would be if the younger generations found the meaning they're seeking
in the way our faith connects to the vital needs of our nation and our
world. I can think of several congregational models that might excite the
curiosity and inspire the inner core of someone who had never before
thought of church service.

- communities that consciously set themselves apart from racist,
  sexist, money-oriented value systems;

- congregations whose members are committed to living out a
  biblical vision of compassion to the poor and outcast; centers of
  spiritual nurture, focusing on personal prayer and other spiritual
  disciplines;

- multicultural communities of faith consciously affirming their
  heterogeneity;

- centers that challenged their members to wholeness of body, mind,
  and spirit with healing services and "laying on of hands."

Would these beacon congregations produce new kinds of leaders for
the church? I believe they would, and the enormous diversity of talents
drawn into clergy ranks would do much to restore a balance among the
various candidate constituencies. Recruiting potential clergy from congregations such as the above would be like fishing in a barrel.

We do in fact have congregations with the characteristics of these
models. They may be few and far between, but they exist. Unfortu-
nately we tend to hold up the typical unassuming and unadventurous
congregation, which may see itself as so beleaguered that it dare not step
out from the crowd.

We do have people in the church who understand the kind of force such churches could have. These are the people I would like to see on recruitment task forces in every denomination. They have no qualms about letting someone know that he or she might make a fine pastor. They enjoy "planting seeds." They want to support those prospective clergy and their families.

I have used the word *recruitment* throughout this book. It was part of our original charge when we began the candidacy study to examine not only how denominations examined and screened their candidates, but how they identified people of promise and stimulated them to consider God's call. Yet the idea of recruitment is controversial in the church world. Here are two expressions of the ambivalence and concern that colors people's perceptions of the dynamics of recruitment.

> We have used the words "recruitment," "selection," and "discern-ment"...often with a sense of dissatisfaction with all of them. The obvious word to use is "call." It is precisely the status of that word, however, that typifies much of the malaise being experienced con-cerning the recruitment-selection-discernment procedure....A voca-tion to the specially focussed ministries of church leadership...has historically required not only a further "inward" call but also a specific call from the church. Confusion over this distinction has created confusion within "the process."...
>
> God does not coerce. Therefore the church should not coerce. The nation conscripts recruits in times of crisis, but the church requires volunteers.[2]

> When God calls a person to leadership and to a particular position in the church, that person must respond....
>
> A person in responding must do so out of the freedom to re-spond. God does not compel. The church cannot compel. Rather God frees people to respond.[3]

It is my contention that our current interpretation of the dynamics of the call leads us into a kind of diffidence or passivity. The idea of re-cruitment to some connotes compelling against one's will. It may also suggest artificially imposed quotas.

Yet what does it take for people to volunteer for anything? First, visible signs of life. Next, solid information about a particular organiza-tion or cause. Along the way, prospects want to connect with people for whom they feel admiration and respect. Finally, they look for more than an invitation; they long for a challenge.

Therefore I propose the following five attributes for a process that reaches out, gathers in, and nurtures the many different kinds of people needed in the church.

1. Sufficient freedom in the system, so that everyone who feels called has the opportunity to explore whether this vocation is right for her or him, having been provided solid, well-presented information.

2. Clarity on the part of middle judicatories (guided by national offices) as to the kinds of individuals who will be needed in their regions for the work of the church in the twenty-first century.

3. Candid dialogue with individuals about the likelihood of ordained ministry for them, with clear signals given to those who do not show promise.

4. Advocacy and support for aspirants—from people other than those who need to be candid and straightforward about perceived liabilities.

5. Clear affirmation to exceptional candidates so that they feel assured that their sacrifices will be rewarded.

I believe these attributes can be factored into any candidacy process, whether it is front-end-loading, middle-loading, or back-end-loading. My bias is not about the timing of a yes or no answer—whether prior, during, or following seminary; I respect the needs of different systems to choose a pattern that fits their polity and culture.

At the end of a five-year exploration of the candidacy scene, I come away with special respect for those hard-working people on Boards of Ordained Ministry, Commissions on Ministry, Multisynodical Candidates Committees, Human Resource Committees, Committees on Ministry, and Committees on Preparation for Ministry. I hope this book is an accurate assessment of your situations, your experiences, and, above all, the concerns and needs you related to our research team.

A key blunder would be to add recruitment functions to your already overloaded agendas. There should be separate task forces appointed solely to reach out and involve prospective candidates.

Parish clergy and congregational leaders need to be energized to do their part. They will need guidance, training, and continuing support. The first order of business is to ensure that they—and the middle judicatories—have reached consensus on the qualities needed for ministry to the congregations in their area from now into the twenty-first century.

I've talked about how such listings are formulated. They do not need to be long. My own list has only five qualities.

1. Deep faith   Obvious reverence for God and an ongoing search for the meaning of life through biblical and historic paradigms.

2. A call   A sense of the need to serve God, along with an understanding of the difference between service as a baptized Christian and as an ordained minister.

3. Leadership potential   Demonstrated leadership ability from other arenas or evidence of that capacity.

4. Communication skills   Enjoyment of contacts with a variety of people and the ability to communicate easily and effectively.

5. Good health   Physical, emotional, and spiritual health, visible in the person's appearance.

Once again, and I cannot say it strongly enough, there is rarely an oversupply of competent, effective clergy. This will continue to be the case if we assume that the task of finding such clergy belongs to someone else. Lest I be accused of not believing in the power of the Holy Spirit to raise up fit women and men for the ordained ministry, I would like to relate a story my father used to tell. My father was a Lutheran preacher who never went into a pulpit without a memorized sermon. So he loved to tell about the pastor who wondered, as he was preparing his sermon for Sunday, whether he could simply rely on the Holy Spirit to tell him what to say on Sunday morning. Instead of preparing a sermon that week, he simply waited until he stood up in the pulpit. It was then that the Holy Spirit spoke to him and said, "You are a lazy dolt. Because of your sloth, you are going to have to suffer the embarrassment of not having a thing to say to your people this morning."

I believe the Holy Spirit will call fit people to ordained ministry, but we must also do our homework. "We must work the works of him who sent me while it is day; night comes when no one can work." (John 9:4) RSV

We still have some daylight left. Let's get to work!

Our Research Process and Its Participants

In 1987 the Arthur Vining Davis Foundations awarded a grant to The Alban Institute to examine the processes by which candidates move from the decision for ordination through various procedures and reviews toward completion of their seminary education. This grant was predicated on an expanding partnership of other funders that in time included the Board for Theological Education of the Episcopal Church, the Siebert Foundation, and individual contributors. A number of seminaries and judicatories also provided housing, conference sites, travel coverage, and other in-kind contributions.

A consulting team of denominational representatives met with Project Director Roy Osward in December 1987 to identify key concerns and develop hypotheses. For their invaluable help in getting this project underway, we wish to thank William Behrens, Margaret Clark, Margaret Graham, Preston T, Kelsey, Ellis Larsen, Ruth Libbey, Catherine Malcolm, Guy Mehl, Rebecca Parker, Edward White, and Bernie Zerkel.

Active inquiry began in early 1988 with visits to the campuses of four seminaries to field-test a questionnaire being developed to poll a national sample of seminarians. Institutions cooperating in this phase of our work were Virginia Theological Seminary, Lancaster Theological Seminary, Wesley Theological Seminary, and Gettysburg Theological Seminary. Our pilot team included Margaret Clark, Linda Kramer, Ellis Larsen, and Burton Newman.

Two conferences of seminary personnel were convened by Roy Oswald in the spring of 1988 to respond to a survey mailed earlier to deans, admissions officers, and faculty. At the East and West Coast meetings, participants discussed the impact of candidacy processes on the students in their institutions. We are particularly grateful to Auburn

Seminary and Pacific School of Religion for their hospitality and good offices in making these conferences possible.

Participants came from twenty-six institutions, including Berkeley Divinity School, Bethany Theological Seminary, Boston University School of Theology, Chicago Theological Seminary, Christian Theological Seminary, Church Divinity School of the Pacific, Concordia Theological Seminary, Drew University Theological Seminary, Eastern Baptist Theological Seminary, Episcopal Theological Seminary of the Southwest, Fuller Theological Seminary, General Theological Seminary, George Mercer, Jr., Memorial School of Theology, Golden Gate Baptist Theological Seminary, Gordon-Conwell Theological Seminary, Harvard Divinity School, Louisville Presbyterian Theological Seminary, Luther Northwestern Theological Seminary, Nashotah House Theological Seminary, New Brunswick Theological Seminary, North Park Theological Seminary, Pacific Lutheran Theological Seminary, Pittsburgh Theological Seminary, Seabury-Western Theological Seminary, Union Theological Seminary, and Union Theological Seminary in Virginia.

By the end of 1988 interviews were underway with bodies generically identified as "screening committees" and with judicatory staffs. Over a two-year period there were twenty-six on-site visits encompassing lay and clergy within nine denominations: American Baptist Churches in the USA, Christian Church (Disciples of Christ), Episcopal, Lutheran (ELCA), Presbyterian (USA), Reformed Church in America, United Church of Christ, Unitarian-Universalist, and United Methodist. In the majority of cases, a four-page questionnaire was sent in advance to committee or commission participants and a representative group was interviewed on-site for two hours. During each visit a bishop, executive, or designee was also interviewed. The questionnaire and the conversations were designed to (1) elicit a clear picture of judicatory procedures for recruitment, screening, and support; (2) encourage candid assessments of the quality and type of candidates produced. Interviewers also sought information from screening personnel as to training, workload, and reporting relationships.

Board for Theological Education funding facilitated interviews with the Episcopal Dioceses of Atlanta, Arizona, California, Chicago, Connecticut, Lexington, Nevada, New Jersey, North Carolina, Pittsburgh, South Dakota, Rhode Island, Texas, and Vermont. The Arthur Vining Davis Foundations grant made possible data gathering from the Central

Florida Presbytery, the Florida United Methodist Conference, the Schenectady Classis of the RCA, The Episcopal Diocese of Atlanta, the Milwaukee Synod ELCA, and the Massachusetts Conference of the UCC.

The interview team assisting Roy Oswald in this phase of the project consisted of Margaret Clark, Antti Lepisto, Lois Simpson, and Edward White. The team also carried out extensive data gathering at four Episcopal seminaries designated by the Board for Theological Education. Berkeley Divinity School, Trinity Episcopal School for Ministry, the Church Divinity School of the Pacific, and Seabury-Western Theological Seminary made it possible for our team to talk to ten to twelve seminarians, a dean, and two faculty members over a two-day period at each campus.

Simultaneously a ten-page questionnaire was developed by Roy Oswald and Dr. Ellis Larsen of Wesley Theological Seminary. Designees at twenty-three seminaries acted as our representatives, distributing surveys to more than 2,700 students. We are grateful to those who assisted us at the following institutions: Berkeley Divinity School, Bexley Hall, Brite Divinity School, Church Divinity School of the Pacific, Chicago Theological Seminary, Columbia Theological Seminary, Duke University Divinity School, Episcopal Divinity School, Episcopal Theological Seminary of the Southwest, Garrett Theological Seminary, General Theological Seminary, Iliff School of Theology, Lexington Theological Seminary, Louisville Theological Seminary, Luther Northwestern Theological Seminary, Nashotah House, School of Theology of the University of the South, Seabury-Western Theological Seminary, Trinity Episcopal School for Ministry, United Theological Seminary of the Twin Cities, Virginia Theological Seminary, Wartburg Theological Seminary, and Wesley Theological Seminary.

Twelve hundred and ninety-seven seminary students completed and returned the questionnaire. Each participating institution received its own individual profile.

In the final stages of this project, The Alban Institute was invited to participate in two conferences of project directors from various Lilly Endowment-sponsored research initiatives. These meetings convened a very diverse cross section of theological and institutional representatives. As this book moves toward publication, Roy Oswald is completing a comparative study of recruitment methods used by three separate Lutheran entities in the state of Wisconsin. This final activity was enabled by a grant from the Siebert Foundation.

Qualities for Ministry Identified by the American Baptist Churches in the USA

In 1988 the American Baptist Churches in the USA (ABC) received a Lilly Endowment grant to help them develop a list of positive qualities for ministry. They were aware of the potential conflict inherent in trying to forge a consensus within a congregationally oriented denomination. Given the autonomy of local congregations, they felt they needed to carry out a wide consultation. The Educational Ministries Office of the ABC held a two-day consultation, bringing together leaders from all sectors of the denomination to define criteria for leadership in ministry.

One of the positive outcomes of the ABC consultation was the strong sense that these characteristics would manifest themselves in different ways with different age groups. It is one thing to think about desired qualities in a fully mature, developed, and effective pastor. But what qualities are desired at earlier stages?

As a result of this type of thinking, the group accepted the challenge of delineating desired qualities within three age categories.

Youth	(ages thirteen to seventeen)
Traditional College Age	(ages eighteen to twenty-two)
Second-Career Candidates	(ages twenty-six to thirty-six)

The following list identifies the qualities they saw desirable in candidates and clues that would indicate the presence of the qualities.

Youth (Ages Thirteen to Seventeen)

As a young person, the potential candidate for ordained ministry

1. Is moving toward being a whole person.

— A person who is developing moral integrity rooted in emotional and social wholeness.

Clues

— Exhibits a sense of self-worth
— Exhibits self-confidence, while admitting limits and vulnerability
— Is able to ask for help and share leadership roles
— Is growing in mind, body, and spirit, and therefore has capacity to care, help, and give
— Displays attitude of joy, hope, and optimism
— Does not need to be self-serving; is flexible and empathic
— Acts fairly and acknowledges when she or he does not
— Treats members of the opposite sex with respect and dignity
— Acknowledges mistakes; seeks forgiveness
— Follows through on accepted responsibilities.

2. Is seeking to know God.

— As a disciple of Christ, a person who engages in a process of formation with the Spirit.

Clues

— Asks theological questions
— Is willing to articulate personal faith
— Tries some devotional practices—Bible reading, prayer
— Participates in Bible study/prayer/support small group(s)
— Is willing to pray aloud in a group
— Asks questions regarding spiritual or faith concerns
— Engages in opportunities for Christian fellowship
— Begins to make connections among biblical faith and personal action and current events.

3. Is a "connected" and relational person.

— A person who seeks to develop relationships with people where each is empowered and the gifts of each are called forth.

Clues

— Exhibits mutuality in family commitment
— Depends on others and is dependable
— Asks for help
— Is intentional about connections to communities of faith (local, regional, national, ecumenical)
— Says "we" not "they"
— Gives his or her time and money
— Knows how to win and how to lose
— Includes new people
— Actively listens to others.

4. Is curious, adventuresome, and creative.

— A person who sees life as a gift and approaches life with respect, curiosity, and joy.

Clues

— Sees beyond the given or obvious
— Connects ideas and realities
— Is more intrigued by possibilities than by givens
— Will not stay discouraged
— Is perceptive, intelligent, and winsome
— Displays energy and enthusiasm
— Is imaginative and creative
— Approaches new experiences with a spirit of adventure
— Is interested in new ideas and activities
— Eats food from different cultures
— Does not put others down
— Enjoys interaction with people of different ages.

5. Is a person of commitment.

   — A person who is willing to engage, with compassion, in the struggle for justice and peace.

   Clues

   — Makes public profession of faith
   — Is an active church member
   — Accepts responsibilities in the church
   — Shows loyalty to congregational life and to the larger body of Christ
   — Brings or invites others to Christ and Christ's church
   — Shows high Christian standards of personal conduct
   — Is aware of international issues and problems
   — Extends care to those who are hurting, lonely, and discouraged
   — Relates well to those who are different from self.

Traditional College Age (Ages Eighteen to Twenty-Two)

1. Possesses a sense of divine presence and calling.

   — A person who evidences potential for a strong personal faith and demonstrates a sense of calling to be a Christian through commit ment to the church and its ministries to the world.

   Clues

   — Spends time in prayer and meditation
   — Engages in reflection on the Scriptures
   — Is perceived by others to be on a "spiritual journey"
   — Identifies with a community of believers and related activities
   — Reads books that deepen his or her understanding of God's will and way
   — Lives with a sense of grace
   — Is willing to raise questions in dialogue with others about the meaning of faith and life
   — Exhibits continuity in decisions made, personal behaviors, and priorities in relation to commitments expressed.

2. Possesses basic communication skills.

— A person who evidences the capacity to express thought and feeling with clarity in spoken and written form so as to inform, enlighten, motivate, and/or challenge and persuade.

Clues

— In written material is well organized and clear
— In formal and informal articulations is informative, enlightened, and motivational
— Is an attentive, active listener
— Is able to summarize and synthesize
— Is able to speak publicly
— Is able to deal with facts and ideas.

3. Possesses personal maturity and ego strength.

— A person who evidences such wholeness and integrity as to be able to live with risk and vulnerability, who evidences self-confidence in an environment of ambiguity.

Clues

— Has a record of trustworthiness
— Rebounds from defeat; has the ability to bounce back
— Shows dependability in work record:
    Relationships upwards, across, and downwards
    Task performance
— Has lasting relationships with individuals and/or groups
— Reflects high moral and spiritual commitments in lifestyle
— Handles rather than dumps problems
— Is willing to be self-critical and to self-disclose
— Is committed to cause(s) greater than self, i.e., social justice, peace, etc

4. Demonstrates leadership skills.

— A person who evidences leadership abilities by demonstrating enthusiasm, initiative, good judgment, and discernment; who commands respect and has the potential for envisioning and developing plans for actions that will make a difference.

Clues

— Has been elected to leadership positions by peers
— Has been selected for leadership roles by faculty and other college, denominational, or church officials
— Has a track record of leadership accomplishments
— Works well with a variety of people
— Has an opinion respected and sought by peers and others
— Has acceptable testing instrument findings
— Is sought out for ideas and problem-solving skills
— Takes responsibility; is accountable
— Encourages group spirit
— Exhibits sense of hopefulness
— Is able to delegate
— Makes decisions and enables others to make decisions
— Shows congruence between words and behavior.

5. Has an inquiring mind.

— A person who evidences a genuine curiosity about life, a love of learning, an ability to think clearly and critically, and the capacity to tolerate ambiguity in the pursuit of truth.

Clues

— Exhibits a range of interests evident in reading breadth and extra-curricular activities
— Has a commendable academic record, recognition, and awards
— Associates well with a range of peers
— Exhibits breadth and depth of conversation
— Is open to and enjoys learning
— Has effective study habits
— Makes informed decisions and applications.

6. Expresses empathic caring.

— A person who evidences potential for empathy and cares for others and self and the structures of society and nature.

Clues

— Displays self-esteem
— Acts out convictions and values
— Shows concern for others
— Is able to give and receive care
— Is concerned about nonviolence
— Thinks about consequences of own actions
— Shows evidence of making commitments to causes, organizations, structures.

Second-Career Candidates (Ages Twenty-six to Thirty-six)

1. Shows a sense of call rooted in a convicted personal devotion to Christ that is expressed in a confident, hopeful, visionary commitment to the church's ministry.

Clues

— Is already actively involved in some form of ministry
— Is in the process of rebuilding life after a crisis
— Exhibits personal relationship with Christ through prayer and devotional life, Bible study
— Positive attitude toward the church as the people of God.

2. Possesses personal qualities and gifts for leadership: intelligence, initiative, analytical ability, appropriate use and confrontation of power, courage, openness to change, ability to communicate and teach, ability to handle conflict.

Clues

— Shows evidence of being a structured leader—indication of this coming from congregation

— Has exhibited leadership in previous careers; shows evidence of
    intentional, ordered progression in career
— Shows good judgment; self-disciplined
— Shows ability to admit error; evidence of self-acceptance
— Exhibits skill in inspiring others.

3. Is skilled in interpersonal relationships, exhibits: love for people,
personal maturity, trustworthiness, integrity, character, flexibility, empathy, teachability, compassion, sense of humor. Is comfortable with
oneself; engaging—winsome.

Clues

— Relates well with diverse groups of people
— Is usually not defensive
— Shows altruistic behavior; is caring; is a good listener
— Is not exploitive
— Is willing to be moved by others.

4. In the context of the ABC as a multiracial, multicultural community,
is prepared to risk seeking to make a prophetic difference in the church
and the world, both locally and globally, in accordance with biblical and
theological foundations.

Clues

— Has shown courage of own convictions in first career (evidence
    of a prophetic stance in prior church-community experiences)
— Values cross-cultural experience.

5. Is committed to empowering and preparing all the people of God for
their ministries in the world and in the church.

Clues

— Has exhibited a sense of ministry as a layperson
— Has been involved in local church's program of lay ministry
— Displays caring concern for all people in need.

Wisconsin Lutherans' Recruitment Strategies

A Siebert Foundation grant helped to fund Alban Institute work with three Lutheran bodies in the state of Wisconsin: Evangelical Lutheran Church in America, the Lutheran Church—Missouri Synod, and the Wisconsin Evangelical Lutheran Synod.

Each church body agreed to form a recruitment task force that I would work with over the course of eighteen months. In phase 1 we were to critique current methods of clergy recruitment. Based on our assessment, we were to create some alternative recruitment strategies. Phase 2 would involve experimenting with these alternatives over the course of one year. Phase 3 would engage each denomination in an evaluation.

The project is still underway, but the following is a summary of findings so far.

ELCA, Milwaukee Synod

This middle judicatory had already formed a separate committee (the Invitation to Service Committee) tasked with recruiting superior candidates for ministry. The screening function within this synod was performed by a separate group made up of the Candidacy Committee and the Multisynod Task Force. The national body had just initiated these committees in all their synods as a result of a Lilly grant on recruitment efforts.

Current Methods

This group already had some things going for them.

1. The Invitation to Service Committee had already published an occasional four-page newsletter titled "Who Me?" Approximately 130 people identified as being potential candidates of the ordained ministry received the newsletter. The following article titles give you a flavor of the newsletter.

> "Do You See a Minister in the Mirror?"
> "What Does a Congregation Look for in a Pastor?"
> "What Should I Take in College if I Want to Go to Seminary?"
> "Road Trip to Luther Northwestern Seminary and Saint Olaf College in Minnesota"
> "Invitation to Service Advocates Ready to Help"

2. Each September the committee scheduled an event for high school students. Held at Carthage College, the five-hour event was fast moving. It included a special video on the ordained ministry, three presenters representing different types of ministry, small-group meetings with mentors and students, dinner, and a worship service. Participants could have their pictures taken—with their faces posed in a body-length poster of a bishop, pastor, etc.

Thirty-five youth participated in the 1991 event. The committee had hoped for seventy-five to one hundred participants.

3. Each winter two clergy take a van full of young people to visit Luther Northwestern Seminary and Trinity Seminary. At Trinity this past winter, the seminary had college youth awaiting the van's arrival with a warm welcome and hot pizza. Another van is available for youth to visit Wartburg Theological Seminary in the spring. Each cluster of congregations in the synod is to have an advocate for the recruitment effort and sign youth up for the above activities.

4. The Invitation to Service Committee also tried to survey all clergy in the synod regarding their efforts in recruiting potential candidates for the ordained ministry. The survey requested names of potential

candidates, potential adult mentors for candidates, and youth directors-advisors. Ninety percent of the clergy did not mail back a completed form.

New Alternatives

Here are some new ideas this committee agreed to try as a result of this consultation.

1. Debrief six clergy in the synod who have been known for their recruitment efforts. This debriefing took place in September 1992. Conclusions from that two-hour session:

   a. Older clergy seemed to be most effective in recruiting aspirants. The two main qualities of these older clergy were vitality and integrity.

   b. These clergy had themselves been pursued to consider the ordained ministry.

   c. These clergy appeared to be well-rounded yet were not afraid to reveal their human side. The more encounters potential aspirants have with these clergy the better, especially in settings where clergy can be real.

   d. The process is long-term. An invitation is made, but then it goes underground. These clergy were patient yet persistent in their invitation to service.

2. Two members of the committee agreed to survey the twenty-eight people currently in the pipeline moving toward ordination to ascertain what motivated them to enter the ordination track. Their findings:

   a. More than half grew up in religious families. They chose to write about this in their autobiography required for further theological study. Fifty percent talked about the strength of their mother's faith.

b. They also said that their church was like home to them. They
had always had a religious identity. They had been active in their
local congregations. The church had always been part of their
lives.

c. There were some who hadn't grown up in church. Many of these
were second-career candidates for ministry. These people had
become active in church later in life.

One candidate grew up as an atheist. He married into the
faith. In this case the church had brought him into the ordained
ministry.

Another candidate returned to church when his first child was
born. Here the pastor was most influential.

Three mentioned Lutheran Campus Ministry as being important to them. Three mentioned professors at church colleges who
had influenced them. One identified a national youth gathering
as a turning point. Another mentioned a particular Sunday
school teacher.

Two talked about internal experiences that had brought
them to this career choice, i.e., religious experience when a
mother had died. Two were children of alcoholics.

In a separate survey of the women in the pipeline, the respondents were influenced mainly by their fathers or their grand-
mothers, not their mothers.

For many second-career women a life crisis such as divorce
was a key factor. Here a counselor was most influential.

3. The Invitation to Service Committee also invited several college chaplains to a two-hour debriefing to explore the possibility of chaplains
becoming more active in the recruitment effort. Seminary recruitment
personnel from two seminaries were also invited, one from Lutheran
School of Theology at Chicago and one from Wartburg Theological
Seminary in Dubuque.

Besides the two seminary recruiters, only two attended the meeting, a professor at a church college and a campus pastor at a secular
university.

The college professor was clear about what to do if someone in
his class showed an interest in the parish ministry; he would direct

them to the proper channels. He did not feel okay about identifying students who had specific talents for parish ministry and challenging them to consider this option.

The campus pastor at the secular university was equally difficult to engage in this task. It was clear he had some unresolved feelings about the denomination's stand on the issue of sexuality. This appeared to be a real impediment to his actively recruiting for the ordained ministry.

4. On the drawing board: a training seminar for selected clergy on how to become more effective at recruiting high-quality candidates for the ordained ministry.

5. Also on the drawing board: a gathering of all the Afro-American clergy in the synod to elicit ideas for better recruitment of minority clergy.

6. A training seminar is planned to help congregational mentors identify young people with high potential for being effective parish clergy. These are to be "silent" recruiters who will track potential candidates for the ordained ministry through their high school, college, and seminary life.

The Lutheran Church—Missouri Synod, South Wisconsin District

In the Lutheran Church—Missouri Synod, the middle judicatory called the district does not engage itself in the screening of candidates for ministry. This remains the sole prerogative of the seminary, which decides who shall be admitted for study and who shall be ordained. As a result, the only task left for the district is to recruit men for the ordained ministry (women are not permitted to study for the ordained ministry) and provide them with financial support. That explains the formation of the Student Aid Committee, tasked with raising money to support seminary students and parochial school teachers (women are recruited as teachers) and to distribute these funds equitably. This committee appointed three persons to work with me on a recruitment task force in response to the Siebert grant.

We devised the following plan of action:

1. We publicized a two-phase training program open to all clergy in the district. The program consisted of two phases. In the first phase, I was to offer an hour-long seminar on new member assimilation. This served as a carrot that hopefully would entice these clergy to engage us on the recruitment effort. In the second phases a brief slide show was presented depicting the need for more intensive recruitment efforts on behalf of members of the district. This was followed by an outline of the types of persons needed for the ordained ministry and parochial school teachers and some ways they might be engaged in thinking about the ordained ministry as a career option.

2. A second training seminar was also conducted for lay leaders in district congregations. These laity were to be "silent recruiters" working within their own congregations. We encouraged them to engage in this task and to meet with us one year later to share their experiences.

3. All potential candidates for ministry were placed on a mailing list and would be sent the bimonthly newsletter titled *Project Samuel,* produced by Concordia College in Saint Paul, Minnesota.

4. Two of the members conducted a church workers' day in the suburbs of Milwaukee in February 1993. The program consisted of some music by a Christian rock band and some sketches of what is involved in becoming a church worker in the synod.

5. A bus tour has been planned for the summer of 1993 which will take interested youth to visit the surrounding church colleges and seminaries.

6. Seven hundred young people from this district attended a mass gathering of young people in New Orleans in 1992. The task force is planning to invite these 700 young people to a district event where they will relive some of the rituals and highlights of the mass gathering and to place before them the need for full-time church workers.

7. In July 1993 the task force will gather representatives of the ten

congregations in the district with significant numbers of Afro-American members in order to begin a strategy for recruiting black students for full-time church work.

The Wisconsin Evangelical Lutheran Synod

As yet this denomination has not experienced a shortage of ordained clergy or parochial school teachers. But because of their size (smaller than the above two denominations) and their accurate record keeping, they are sure they will experience a shortage of both by the end of the decade.

This denomination finds no need to do psychological testing of its candidates for ministry as it tracks them right from confirmation age, through their parochial school years, through their time at the denominational college and seminary. This denomination also does not admit women to study for the ordained ministry and up to now has not worked with second-career students.

In my consultations with them, I was able to provide information related to second-career students for the ordained ministry. Together we worked on possible ways to recruit second-career students.

It was a good feeling to actually begin working with people in getting a recruitment agenda moving on a middle judicatory level. In the past two years of this research there was precious little evidence that denominations were engaging in any substantive recruitment effort.

The Siebert Foundation Study yielded the following learnings.

1. The study reminded me of how difficult it is to get a recruitment effort going when most people think there is an oversupply of clergy. The Milwaukee Synod of the ELCA, as a metropolitan synod, usually had more clergy trying to get into their synod than they could use. It is in such places as rural North and South Dakota or rural Montana that it is difficult to get enough clergy to meet the demands of local churches.

2. If it weren't for women and second career students, many of our mainline denominations would be facing a critical shortage of seminary students. The Milwaukee Synod, ELCA, had an oversupply of clergy because it was open to admitting both into their ordination track. The

Lutheran Church–Missouri Synod is facing a shortage of seminarians mainly because they were not admitting women into the ordination track. The Wisconsin Evangelical Lutheran Church was heading into the shortage of seminarians because they not only refused to allow women into the ordination track, but, in addition, up until this year they had not admitted second career students into their seminary.

3. Clergy in a long pastorate have a clear advantage in the recruitment effort. These clergy have lived with the families in their congregations a decade or more and are much more knowledgeable about the quality of family life that surrounded young people, having watched these young people grow up in the church.

4. The study reminded me once again of how little thought has been given to the qualities a middle judicatory should look for in potential candidates for ministry. In all three church bodies, I had to prompt them to see if they could agree on five basic qualities to look for in aspirants. It was almost as though the desired qualities were so obvious that this question did not merit any committee discussion time. All assumed they would recognize a superior candidate when they saw one.

In addition, in all three church bodies the middle judicatory executive had not given these screening committees any direction as to the types of candidates he thought were needed in their system. Once again it was as though these executives assumed that these committee members knew exactly what the region needed in terms of ordained clergy. As a result, each committee member brought his or her own individual assumption about effective clergy to the task.

APPENDIX IV

Strategies for Recruitment
of Minority Candidates

We mainline Protestant denominations increasingly value having multi-cultural congregations. Some of this has to do with our desire to grow and survive. By the turn of the century, for example, California will have more Hispanics and Orientals than persons of European descent. Shortly after the year 2000, over one-third of the U. S. population will be Hispanic. If our congregations are to be relevant to their changing neighborhoods, they must begin now to reach out to nonwhite non-European groups. This is unlikely to happen unless we are inviting Hispanic, Afro-American, and Oriental persons into leadership roles within our denominations.

Yet our desire for more heterogeneous congregations also grows out of our values and theology. Multicultural congregations more fully represent our desired witness to a world torn apart by racial and religious factions. It no longer feels good for the 11:00 a.m. Sunday morning worship service to be the most segregated hour of the entire week. From a pedagogic perspective, we want our children and adult parishioners to learn to live and work in harmony with people of other cultures and races. We want to be about the work of reconciliation, of healing the racial and cultural pain so evident on our continent.

Yet these issues introduce the paradox of many of our white, liberal congregations. We uphold the value of multiculturalism yet seem impotent to achieve it. I recall working in a large, successful, urban Unitarian-Universalist congregation; the congregational leaders were obviously pained over the fact that they could not attract Afro-Americans into membership. Becoming a multicultural congregation was a central component in their mission statement. They had a hard time seeing that their worship service—intellectual and esoteric sermons, accompanied by high-brow hymns and classical choir anthems, attended by people who enjoy cerebral worship, executed precisely within one hour—had little appeal to the majority of Afro-Americans in their neighborhood. (I don't want to engage in stereotyping; some minorities clearly prefer this kind of worship service to any other.)

How much are we asking minority persons to give up to become part of our congregational communities? Or vice versa, how much are we willing to give up to have minorities become part of our congregations? Just as local congregations need to weigh the price of growth, so also denominations need to question whether they are ready and willing to pay the price to grow in the direction of multiculturalism.

Institutional Strategy

One clear way for a denomination to become more multicultural is to invite talented and committed minority men and women into ordained roles. On the first leg of our research on recruitment and screening, I found the six denominations under study despairing in their attempts to recruit qualified and committed minorities into their ordination tracks. Later, during the last phase of our work, when I was working with the three Lutheran denominations in Wisconsin, I realized that *recruiting* capable and committed minorities might be the easiest part of becoming more multicultural. Making the systemic changes necessary to retain them and see that they have a fighting chance to succeed within denominational structures may be our tougher task.

For recruiting and keeping these candidates, we need a denominational strategy at the national level and a second, middle-judicatory strategy. My key learnings came out of the Milwaukee Synod of the ELCA. Denominationally the ELCA has made a commitment to become more multicultural—first by calling people of color into key positions of authority in its national structure. Each decision-making unit at the national level is to include minority consultation. When the Milwaukee Synod began reaching out to Afro-American candidates for ministry, these men and women could consult with Afro-American personnel at the national level.

Another key building block in the Milwaukee strategy was hiring Kenneth Wheeler, a competent, attractive, committed Afro-American pastor as a staff member of the synod. Through my research within this synod, I was able to debrief two Afro-American candidates about to be ordained into parish ministry. I was impressed with the talent, attractiveness, and commitment of these two candidates. Both were coming into the ELCA from other denominational traditions. Both seemed happy to be welcomed into a mainline denominational tradition. Growing out of my work with this synod, what follows is my sense of the key components needed to effect a denominational strategy for inviting minorities into the ordained ministry within our mainline denominations.

Foundational Building Blocks

1. *Minority personnel in key leadership positions.* Minorities need to see persons of color in positions of authority throughout your system. This means having minority persons on seminary and college faculties (if candidates are being sent to church-related schools). They also need to see that persons of color are holding national and regional staff positions. Without these symbols within your system, these minorities may not see much future for themselves within your denomination.

2. *Minority-specific recruitment teams.* Initial contacts with potential minority candidates need to come from people of their own race and culture. Do not expect that one multicultural committee will deal with Afro-American, Hispanic, and Hmong prospects. Each of these races and cultures, so different from the others, needs a specific, unique strategy for success.

The Milwaukee Synod (ELCA) had ordained clergy of all three of the above-mentioned minorities: Afro-American, Hispanic, and Hmong. One afternoon the synod's Invitation to Service Committee interviewed a Hmong pastor and two Afro-American candidates. The difference between the two cultures could not have been more striking. The Hmong pastor talked about how difficult it was for the Hmong people to adjust to certain aspects of Lutheran worship. They are not used to participating in worship. They come to listen and receive. He talked about their reticence in reciting the creed, saying the Lord's Prayer out loud, or reading a confession of faith. The Hmong pastor himself was a quiet, soft-spoken, nonassertive male. Compare this to some of the freedom often expressed in certain Afro-American services, where members at any point are likely to shout, "Amen, Sister" or "Praise the Lord." These congregations usually prefer their clergy to be charismatic, assertive, and confident. Hispanic worship has yet another set of norms and customs.

I'm recommending a culture- and race-specific task force of three or more members who would develop a strategy for attracting one of their own into the denominational system. This group may be accountable to a large recruitment task force but would not need to attend all of the larger group's meetings. Several times a year the small group would report on their strategy and progress.

3. *Clarity of motivation for inviting minorities into your ordained ministry.* Too often we want ordained minority persons within our denominations so they will revitalize our dying urban congregations. To be sure, some may be called to this ministry. Others may not. We often set these people up for failure by sending them into some of our toughest places without giving them adequate support or resources. We then brand them as incompetent when they cannot work miracles.

Minority clergy want the same options offered other clergy within your system. Some might like to serve in thriving suburban parishes or on the staff of large congregations. As minorities consider joining the ranks of clergy in your denomination, they need to see possibilities for personal success within your system.

Student Recruitment

If you're going to mine for gold, you need to go where it can be found—to riverbeds where it has been found. A number of evangelical nondenominational colleges, Bible colleges, and seminaries have had success recruiting minority students. Why not go to these campuses looking for ordination candidates for mainline denominations?

The Christian College Coalition, 329 Eighth Street, N.E., Washington, DC 20002, offers a "Racial and Ethnic College Inventory," a list of more than eighty evangelical liberal arts colleges. For each school the listing includes the percentage of minority students, broken into categories: Native American, Afro-American, Hispanic, Oriental, foreign white.

The American Association of Bible Colleges, P.O. Box 1523,

Fayetteville, AR 72702, has a directory of more than one hundred Bible colleges (but no statistics as to minority student populations).

Most evangelical colleges and nondenominational seminaries are happy to have mainline denominations recruit from their campuses. But I don't advise sending a representative to a vocations or recruitment day (with minority recruitment in mind) unless you have in place the minority-specific task force mentioned earlier. Know what minorities you want to target; allow students of that group to talk candidly to one or more clergy of their race or culture. They need answers to the critical question: What is it like to work in the denomination?

Following is a partial list of evangelical, nondenominational Bible colleges and seminaries with significant minority populations. Undergraduate students from these colleges could be encouraged to attend your denominational seminaries. (Before you recruit, have some understandings with your seminaries as to whether or not the particular Bible college's degree meets seminary entrance requirements.) Students at (graduates of) nondenominational seminaries would need minimal additional training.

Bible Colleges

Philadelphia College of Bible
200 Langhorne Manor
Langhorne, PA 19047-2992
estimate: 20 percent minority status

Washington Bible College
6511 Princess Garden Parkway
Lanham, MD 20706
800-787-0256
estimate: 40-45 percent minority status

Moody Bible Institute
820 North LaSalle Boulevard
Chicago, IL 60610
800-333-3139
estimate: 2 percent minority status

Nondenominational Seminaries

Capital Theological Seminary
6511 Princess Garden Parkway
Lanham, MD 20706
800-787-0256
estimate: 40 percent of minority status

Dallas Theological Seminary
3909 Swiss Avenue
Dallas, TX 75204
800-992-0998
estimate: 10 percent minority status

Fuller Theological Seminary
135 North Oakland Avenue
Pasadena, CA 91182
800-235-2222
estimate: 47 percent ethnic population (6 percent Afro-American)

Gordon-Conwell Theological Seminary
130 Essex Street
South Hamilton, MA 01982
800-428-7329

Talbort Theological Seminary
13800 Biola Avenue
La Mirada, CA 90639-0001
800-OK-BIOLA
49 percent ethnic (47 Afro-American students)

Does this sound more like a football draft than recruitment for the ordained ministry? To be sure, this may feel as if we are stealing talent from other Christian churches. We need to be sensitive about that. When we recruit for ordination candidates at these colleges and seminaries we are simply offering these minorities a choice. If they have a better offer elsewhere, they will not join us. In the long run they will not stay with our denominations if they experience the same racial tension that blocks them out of so much else in our society.

Until we have a critical mass of minorities within our judicatories from which we can recruit our own minority candidates, we will need to import some from outside our systems.

What Do We Have to Offer?

You may be asking what we mainline Protestants have to offer evangelical blacks or other minorities. In fact, we may have more to offer than we realize.

Several years ago a new association was formed, the National Black Association of Evangelicals (NBAE), an offshoot of the National Association of Evangelicals (NAE). This division came about largely because the Afro-American community felt the NAE was not showing adequate concern for the urban poor.

What does this mean for mainline denominations? If we are clear about our agenda for the urban poor, we have a definite point of connection with the Afro-American evangelical community. Our social agenda is to our advantage.

Another advantage is the structure of our denominational networks. Many of the students attending evangelical, nondenominational colleges, Bible colleges, and seminaries come from nondenominational congregations. When you are not tied to a denominational network, what are your chances of finding a pulpit of your own? You often start by finding a congregation of your own, possibly a storefront church, or wait for a call from a nondenominational congregation. Only pastors who are politically well-connected get calls to significant congregations. The denominational structure that helps manage congregational calls is one feature that might make our mainline systems attractive.

Why the Evangelicals?

Evangelical minority students have some desirable qualities for ministry not found in more liberal circles. To begin with, most have had a powerful transformational religious experience. They will have an advantage over our mainline seminary graduates, who may have little training or experience in transformational spirituality.

We are talking about conversion. In my seminary training I certainly was not given any guidelines for how to pray someone through a conversion experience. I was taught to be a caretaker of souls who had already undergone conversion somewhere else. For the most part I was taught how to care for those baptised into the faith—people who may never have had a religious transformational experience.

A second possible benefit of these evangelical minority candidates is that they often know a lot more than liberals about how to grow a congregation. More than likely they were converted and nurtured in a thriving, growing church.

How Will Evangelical Minorities Fit into our Denominations Theologically?

According to my Afro-American friend Robin Bell, who taught me much of the above and who came into the ELCA clergy from the nondenominational Dallas Theological Seminary, they fit in better than we might expect. Robin claims that John Calvin and Martin Luther were the theologians most studied in his systematic theology courses.

Styles of worship might be a more difficult issue for these minorities than theology. To what extent will we grant them a modicum of freedom related to worship and liturgy? To quote Robin, "I have often wondered how much I needed to sell my soul to Lutheran liturgy in order to serve within the Lutheran church. From my perspective as a Lutheran pastor, we need to be freed ourselves from some of our forms of worship. If non-Christians show a desire to belong to our congregations, do we insist that they learn to sing sixteenth-century hymns? This can be a real barrier to new Christians. Can we even think of having drums, guitars, and keyboards in our churches along with our grand pipe organs? Is inflexibility of worship style so important? If we are in agreement theologically, do we need to be so similar in our hymnody and liturgical movement? Who knows—some of our old-time members just might enjoy a little more life and soul in their Sunday-morning worship."

Why Is Minority Recruitment Important?

At this point in history we have a window of opportunity to be much
more multicultural in our congregations. It's time we intentionally
worked with minorities inside our systems, allowing them to teach us
how we might become truly multicultural and inclusive. But how can
this happen if we don't have those minorities in our systems? If we don't
have them, we must try harder to find them, as our theology demands
that we share our ministry with all of God's children.

Chapter II

1. Constant H. Jacquet, ed., *Yearbook of American and Canadian Churches 1992* (Nashville: Abingdon, 1992), 285.

2. Seminary survey conducted by Roy Oswald and Ellis Larsen for the Board for Theological Education of the Episcopal Church, 1989.

3. Joseph O'Neill and Richard Murphy, "Changing Age and Gender Profiles among Entering Seminary Students: 1975-1989," *Ministry Research Notes* (Spring 1991): 3.

4. Ibid., 8.

5. Gene I. Maeroff, ed., *Sources of Inspiration* (Kansas City, MO.: Sheed and Ward, 1992), v.

6. Jerilee Grandy and Mark Greiner, "Academic Preparation of Master of Divinity Candidates," *Ministry Research Notes* (Fall 1990): 7.

7. O'Neill and Murphy, "Changing Age and Gender Profiles," 2.

8. Grandy and Greiner, "Academic Preparation," 8.

9. L. Guy Mehl, "The Quality of Ministerial Candidates from a Counselor's Perspective," mimeographed (Lancaster, PA: Lancaster Career Development Center, March 12, 1991), 4-5.

10. Peter Steinfels, "Shortage of Qualified New Clergy Causing Alarm for U. S. Religion," *New York Times*, 9 July 1989, A-1.

11. Paul Wilkes, "The Hands That Would Shape Our Souls," *Atlantic Monthly* (December 1990): 71.

12. O'Neill and Murphy, "Changing Age and Gender Profiles," 10.

13. Mehl, "Quality of Ministerial Candidates," 3.

14. O'Neill and Murphy, "Changing Age and Gender Profiles," 8.

15. E. Larsen and J. Shopshire, "A Profile of Contemporary Seminarians," *Theological Education*, Vol. 24, No. 2 (Spring 1988): 10-136.

16. "Background Report," Recruitment and Selection Committee (A-183), Board for Theological Education of the Episcopal Church, 1990, 6.

17. Brooke A. Masters, "'Post-Bac' Students Pursue Their Med School Dreams," *Washington Post*, 30 April 1993, D-6.

18. Constant H. Jacquet, ed., *Yearbook of American and Canadian Churches 1991* (Nashville: Abingdon, 1991), 286-87.

19. "The Unchurched America—10 Years Later," a report, Princeton, N.J.: Princeton Research Center for the Study of Religion, 1988.

20. Kevin Matthews, "Clergy Deployment Issues," in "WECA Newsletter" 14 no. 7, mimeographed at Holy Trinity Parish, Bowie, MD (1989): 2.

21. Barbara G. Wheeler, "What Kind of Leadership for Tomorrow's Churches?" *Action Information* (November-December 1985): 9.

22. Wilkes, "Hands That Would Shape Our Souls," 80.

23. Ibid., 81.

24. O'Neill and Murphy, "Changing Age and Gender Profiles," 5.

25. "New MDs: Up to Their Ears in Debt," *Washington Post*, 23 March 1993, Health-5. Cited statistics from the Association of American Medical Colleges.

Chapter III

1. "Theological Education for Ministry in the ELCA," Task Force on Theological Education, August 1991.

2. D. Hoge, J. Carroll, and F. Scheets, *Patterns of Parish Leadership: Cost and Effectiveness in Four Denominations* (Kansas City, MO: Sheed and Ward, 1988), 7.

3. "Theological Education for Ministry in the ELCA."

4. Robert Wood Lynn, "Coming Over the Horizon," in *Good Stewardship: A Handbook for Seminary Trustees*, ed. Barbara E. Taylor and Malcolm L. Warford (Washington, DC: Association for Governing Boards, 1991), 59.

5. Ibid., 63.

6. John C. Fletcher, "Living Creatively beyond Survival: The Coming Crisis for Theological Seminaries," *Action Information* (November-December 1980): 10.

Chapter IV

1. Hartley Hall, "Call to Ministry," cited in *Bits and Pieces #3*, Study to Enrich Inquirers and Candidates (SEIC), Presbyterian Church (USA) (1990), 1.
   2. O'Neill and Murphy, "Changing Age and Gender Profiles," 4.
   3. Gene I. Maeroff, ed., *Sources of Inspiration* (Kansas City, MO.: Sheed and Ward, 1992), 5-6.
   4. Arlin Rothauge, *Sizing Up a Congregation for New Member Ministry* (New York: The Episcopal Church Center, 1983.
   5. Hoge, Carroll, and Scheets, *Patterns of Parish Leadership*, 10.
   6. "Call System Proposal," rev. ed., Call System Task Force, Presbyterian Church (USA), January 1992, 8.
   7. Roy Oswald, *North Indiana Conference Small Congregation Study* (Washington, DC: The Alban Institute, 1988).
   8. Hoge, Carroll, and Scheets, *Patterns of Parish Leadership*, 7-8.

Chapter V

1. O'Neill and Murphy, "Changing Age and Gender Profiles," 12.
   2. *Manual on Ministry: Perspectives and Procedures for Ecclesiastical Authorization of Ministry* (St. Louis: Office for Church Life and Leadership, United Church of Christ, 1991).
   3. Jerilee Grandy and Mark Greiner. "Academic Preparation of Master of Divinity Candidates," *Ministry Research Notes* (Fall 1990): 12.
   4. O'Neill and Murphy, "Changing Age and Gender Profiles," 8.
   5. Paul Wilkes, "The Hands That Would Shape Our Souls," *Atlantic Monthly* (December 1990): 84.
   6. Donald Hands and Wayne Fehr, *Spiritual Wholeness for Clergy: A New Psychology of Intimacy with God, Self, and Others* (Washington, DC: The Alban Institute, 1993), 61.

Chapter VI

1. Kurtis C. Hess, "The Crisis in the Placement System of the Presbyterian Church (USA/)," *As I See It Today* 2, no. 5, (December 1988).

2. Carlos Wilton, in *Presbyterian Outlook,* September 1989, cited in "A Possible Shortage of Ministers," *Bits and Pieces #2,* Study to Enrich Inquirers and Candidates (SEIC), Presbyterian Church (USA) (1990).

3. Hoge, Carroll, and Scheets, *Patterns of Parish Leadership,* 7-10.

4. Ibid., 138.

5. George H. Gallup, Jr., and Robert Bezilla, Religious News Service, "Protestant Denominations Highly Diverse, Poll Finds," *Washington Post,* 27 March 1993, B-1.

6. Dr. John Cassell, Bethany Theological Seminary (unpublished transcript approved for publication).

7. O'Neill and Murphy, "Changing Age and Gender Profiles," 12.

8. Gustav Niebuhr, "Arlington Priest Cultivates Bumper Crop of Catholic Seminarians," *Washington Post,* 27 December 1992, A-3.

9. Ibid.

10. *Bits and Pieces #1,* Study to Enrich Inquirers and Candidates (SEIC), Presbyterian Church (USA) (1990). Statistics cited from Office of Preparation for Ministry, Church Vocations Ministry Unit, PC (USA).

11. O'Neill and Murphy, "Changing Age and Gender Profiles," 3-4.

12. Ibid., 4.

13. Jacquet, *Yearbook of American and Canadian Churches 1990,* 274.

14. George W. Cornell, Associated Press, "Despite Southern Baptist Leaders' Opposition, Female Clergy Increasing," *Dallas Morning News,* 8 May 1993.

15. O'Neill and Murphy, "Changing Age and Gender Profiles," 4-5.

16. Jacquet, *Yearbook of American and Canadian Churches 1990,* 276.

17. Paul Wilkes, "The Hands That Would Shape Our Souls," *Atlantic Monthly* (December 1990): 81.

18. O'Neill and Murphy, "Changing Age and Gender Profiles," 5.

19. Ibid., 4. Statistics cited from the National Center for Education Statistics.

20. Peter Steinfels, "Shortage of Qualified New Clergy Causing Alarm for U.S. Religion," *New York Times,* 9 July 1989, A-1.

21. James E. Annand, "Statement to the House of Bishops from Council of Deans of Episcopal Seminaries," in "Leaven" 27, no. 7, mimeographed newsletter, National Network of Episcopal Clergy Associations (December 1987): 1.

22. Donald Hands and Wayne Fehr, *Spiritual Wholeness for Clergy: A New Psychology of Intimacy with God, Self, and Others* (Washington, DC: The Alban Institute, 1993), 9.

23. Donald R. Hands, "Towards Liberation from Shamed Sexuality," *Action Information* (May-June 1991): 12.

24. Lloyd Rediger, *Ministry and Sexuality* (Minneapolis: Fortress, 1990), quoted in James A. Sparks, Robert O. Ray, and Donald C. Houts, "Sexual Misconduct in Ministry: What Clergy at Risk Are Doing about It," *Congregations* (November-December 1992): 6.

25. Gustav Niebuhr, "Sexual Abuse by Priests Called a Historic Crisis," *Washington Post*, 27 March 1993, B-7.

26. Sparks, Ray, and Houts, "Sexual Misconduct in Ministry," 7.

27. Annand, "Statement to the House of Bishops," 2.

28. John C. Fletcher, "Living Creatively beyond Survival: The Coming Crisis for Theological Seminaries," *Action Information* (November-December): 9.

Chapter VII

1. Hoge, Carroll, and Scheets, *Patterns of Parish Leadership*. Toll-free order number: 1-800-333-7373.

2. Masthead of *Bits and Pieces*, Study to Enrich Inquirers and Candidates (SEIC), Presbyterian Church (USA).

3. The Study to Enrich Inquirers and Candidates (SEIC) Project, c/o Richard M. Webster, Project Director, Room M-063, 100 Witherspoon Street, Louisville, KY 40202-1396.

4. "Background Report," Recruitment and Selection Committee (A-183), Board for Theological Education of the Episcopal Church, 1990, 22.

5. "Call System Proposal," rev. ed., Call System Task Force, Presbyterian Church (USA), January 1992, 50-53.

6. Seminary survey conducted by Roy Oswald and Ellis Larsen for the Board for Theological Education of the Episcopal Church, 1989.

7. Jerilee Grandy and Mark Greiner, "Academic Preparation of master of Divinity Candidates," *Ministry Research Notes* (Fall 1990): 10.

8. "Ministry Losing Prestige?" *The Lutheran* (28 February 1990).

9. Hoge, Carroll, and Scheets, *Patterns of Parish Leadership.*

10. Jacqueline McMakin and Sonja Dyer, *Working from the Heart* (San Diego: LuraMedia, 1989).

Chapter VIII

1. Peter L. Benson and Carolyn H. Ecklin, eds., *Effective Christian Education: A National Study of Protestant Congregations* (Minneapolis: Search Institute, 1990).

2. "Background Report," Recruitment and Selection Committee (A-183), Board for Theological Education of the Episcopal Church, 1990, 19.

3. "Call System Proposal," rev. ed., Call System Task Force, Presbyterian Church (USA), January 1992, 8.